WAY with WORDS

David Shayer

Evans

Evans Brothers Limited

Introduction

Ways with Words is written for teachers of children in the age range 9–13 years (Key Stages 2 and 3) and provides resources and teaching ideas which will allow the requirements of the National Curriculum to be met in the area of Knowledge About Language, a knowledge which children must begin to acquire in the primary school.

English 5–16 recommends a fieldwork approach to language, with children collecting their own data which is . . . 'all around once teachers and pupils know what to look for'. It is intended that these activity-based units will stimulate just this kind of 'collecting' approach and create opportunities for lively talk and writing as well as providing insight into the workings of language and helping vocabulary development.

In preparing the activities two sections in particular of *English 5–16* have been kept in mind: 'Linguistic terminology' and 'Knowledge about language'. These sections recommend that pupils encounter and understand such things as loan words, word structures, Latinate words, puns, synonymy, historical variants, word games, nonsense words, names and origins of surnames, brand names, euphemisms, and words from inventions. An old-fashioned 'grammar' approach to these concepts is the last thing that is needed, and the units are based on the assumption that finding out about these things can be entertaining and involve children in lively and stimulating activities.

Some units are harder than others, and almost all can be modified up or down a scale of difficulty. Group or paired work and class discussions are integral to all activities.

English 5–16 repeatedly refers to the need for general stimulation and arousal of interest, and it is my intention to achieve this; and while it is undesirable to tie each activity to a specific attainment target, the activities lead directly to the Knowledge About Language requirements incorporated into each of the Targets at levels 5, 6 and 7 within Key Stages 2 and 3.

David Shayer
Caerleon 1990

Contents

1 Colours

Tell the children that the human eye can distinguish thousands of colours, but we have words for only about 200.

Ask the children how many colours they can name. Together, make up a list (use objects in the room to give ideas). Sort the colours into groups: types of red, yellow, green etc. (Children can underline colours of the same 'family' with a coloured pen.)

Now make a large board with the main colour names in a row at the top (appropriately coloured and decorated). Give the children a week to find as many colour names as possible, write them on slips of paper and stick them on the board under the right heading. Count how many words have been added each day.

At the end of the week count the total for each colour, count the overall total, and find which colour has most variants (a graph could be made). Target: to find 40 or 50 in total.

Teacher's list

WHITE: silver, snow-white, chalk-white, pearl, cream, lily-white, milk-white, white as a sheet, alabaster, ivory, Chinese white, off-white.

BLACK: ebony, inky black, soot-black, jet-black, charcoal, pitch-black, coal-black, raven.

GREY: dove-grey, silver-grey, oyster-grey, lead, battleship-grey, gull-grey, mouse-grey, slate, ash, gunmetal, steel-grey.

BROWN: chocolate, cinnamon, rust, bronze, tan, hazel, khaki, cocoa-brown, coffee, nut-brown, fawn, umber, sepia, terracotta, mahogany, auburn, russet, liver-brown, copper, chestnut, ochre, bistre, beige, autumn leaf brown, biscuit, sand, amber.

RED: scarlet, crimson, vermilion, carnation, carmine, flame, cerise, magenta, cardinal, cherry, ruby, claret, brick, lobster-red, blood-red, coral, pink, salmon-pink, poppy-red, pillarbox red.

ORANGE: marigold, tangerine, apricot, peach, carrot, ginger.

YELLOW: lemon, saffron, sulphur, gold, canary-yellow, primrose, straw-yellow, topaz, crocus-yellow.

GREEN: emerald, jade, grass-green, olive, sage, apple-green, pea-green, bottle-green, moss-green, sea-green, turquoise.

BLUE: azure, peacock-blue, sky-blue, navy, royal blue, sapphire blue, robin's egg blue, aquamarine, cornflower, electric blue, indigo, midnight blue, cobalt, powder blue.

PURPLE: violet, lavender, plum, maroon, lilac, mauve, amethyst, damson, burgundy, puce.

Help the children with the more difficult names by trying to find an object which is a good example of the colour.

Further activities

1. The children collect some paint colour charts from a decorating shop and sort these under colour headings or try to improve on the names given to the colours.

2. Experimenting with some primary colour paints, try to 'invent' a new colour and give it a name.

3. Choose a colour, e.g. red or blue. Find as many objects as you can which are different shades of that colour. How many can you find, 10, 20? Do we have enough words to describe them? What might these be?

4. Write a short description of a brilliantly coloured tropical scene with sea, beach, jungle, fruit, and birds. Use as many colour words as possible, but *not* red, blue, green, yellow, purple, orange, brown, white or black.

2 Multiple Meanings

Give the children the following words and ask them how many meanings they can think of for each:

1. BAR (iron, pub, musical unit, barrier, sandbank, a line across a shield, to which barristers are called, addition to a medal)
2. BRIDGE (across a river, card game, of nose, on a ship, holding false teeth, support for a snooker cue, of a violin)
3. PITCH (football or cricket ground, tar, to throw, to put up a tent, musical note, movement of ship, street vendor's spot)

Discuss and give help.

Point out that one word can have several meanings. Working in pairs or groups, and using dictionaries if desired, give the children 15 minutes to collect as many meanings as possible for each of the following. Set a target of, say, 20 over all.

1. BANK (for money, of river, plane tilt, row of things, for bottles, a mass of cloud, a slope, an undersea sand bar)
2. BEAT (to hit, rhythm, police route, tired, score victory over)
3. CHARGE (cost, forward attack, of electricity, accusation)
4. FACE (front of head, of coal seam, of watch/clock, side of a playing card, to stand up to something, to shape stone)
5. RANGE (distance a bullet can reach, place where guns are fired, stove, to move around widely, line of mountains, to put in rows)
6. KEY (of a door, piano or typewriter, explanation of a map or chart, sycamore fruit, musical scale).

Total 34 (there may be more). Groups/pairs report back.

Game

Play this between two groups; no dictionaries are allowed. Teacher writes down 20 words on slips of paper and puts them in a hat. Group A draws a word and then has one minute to list as many meanings as possible. The total is noted. Group B draws another word and also has one minute to find as many meanings as they can. Their total is noted. Highest score wins, but if the losers can find more meanings for their opponents' word, these are added to their score. Teacher referees; do be generous, e.g. allow the verb 'to fish' and the noun 'a fish' to count as two.

Examples of words

1. BEAM (piece of timber, moon ray, sun ray, light ray, radio signal, to smile, width of a boat)
2. BOLT (of door, crossbow arrow, to lock up, to run away, to swallow quickly, a roll of cloth)
3. CAST (of a play, to throw, to shape in metal, of worms, plaster mould, squint)
4. CELL (of prison, battery, of living matter, monk's)
5. CAPITAL (letter, chief city, sum of money, top of a column)
6. DEGREE (of temperature, of angle, qualification)
7. DRIFT (of snow, to wander, to float on the tide, meaning/intention)
8. FOLD (for sheep, to double over)
9. FRAME (of picture, to wrongly accuse, of a bike, a structure, to see within a photographic rectangle, snooker ball holder, for vegetable-growing)
10. HAND (body part, measure of horse, factory worker, cards dealt, to give help, applause)
11. LITTER (discarded paper, puppies, carrying frame)
12. MINT (herb, to make a coin, sweet, brand new)
13. ORDER (to put in sequence, request for meal, civil honour, to command, quietness)
14. PELT (with rain, to throw, animal fur, to run fast)
15. RACE (of humans, running competition, nationality, fiercely flowing water, to run or drive fast)
16. SCALE (musical, of fish, to climb, on weighing machine, map measurement, to scrape off teeth)
17. SEAL (sea animal, wax blob, to make watertight)
18. SET (in tennis, to mend a bone, to make firm, to arrange to music, to go below the horizon, group, collection)

Further activities

1. Find more words that have more than one meaning.
2. *Either* (easier)

   Write two newspaper advertisements, giving lots of detail, for both meanings of the following words:

   > bats, tapes, glasses, iron, sponges, bulbs, tanks

   Or (harder)

   One half of the class attaches specific meanings to words in the list below and writes adverts offering them for sale in the local paper. Start 'FOR SALE . . .'. However, the precise nature of the object is left completely unclear. The idea is to include as much as possible while staying ambiguous.

   The other half of the class then answers the adverts, also electing particular meanings and stating the qualities they hope the object possesses. See if any match.

   > bats, nails, covers, tapes, plugs, glasses, pens, iron, blocks, drums, sponges, bulbs, pipes, tanks.

3 American English

Ask the children if they know where America is. Can anyone say something in an American accent? What kinds of words do Americans use? (E.g. sure thing, gee, cool it, hi, you bet.)

Explain that American English is sometimes quite different from the English we speak in Britain.

Give the children some or all of the following and tell them to complete it by circling. Work in pairs.

American words

Put a circle round the word you think it means

ANTENNA   1. ant's nest   2. *car aerial*   3. fly's leg
APARTMENT   1. cupboard   2. room   3. *flat*
ASH CAN   1. rubbish dump   2. *dustbin*   3. flower pot
BATH ROBE   1. *dressing gown*   2. shower curtain   3. mat
BILLFOLD   1. poster   2. *wallet*   3. paper clip
BLOOPER   1. a bird   2. car horn   3. *a silly mistake*
BRONX CHEER   1. a drink   2. *a rude noise*   3. a song
BROWNIE   1. girl scout   2. a fruit   3. *chocolate biscuit*
BRUNCH   1. crunch   2. *a meal*   3. bunch
CATSUP   1. *tomato sauce*   2. cat bowl   3. accident
CHECKERS   1. policeman   2. straps   3. *game of draughts*
CLUNKER   1. shovel   2. *old car*   3. coal
DOWNSPOUT   1. rain storm   2. umbrella   3. *drainpipe*
DRAPES   1. *curtains*   2. trousers   3. blinds
FAUCET   1. a stream   2. water pipe   3. *a tap*
FREEBEE   1. a game   2. *free gift*   3. lucky
GAS   1. *petrol*   2. gas   3. steam
HANG LOOSE   1. cover up   2. be tired   3. *relax*
HORNSWOGGLE   1. tie up   2. kick   3. *to fool*
ICE BOX   1. *fridge*   2. prison   3. ice-cream machine
JAM   1. jam   2. *jelly*   3. syrup
JELLY   1. *jam*   2. jelly   3. glue
KLUTZ   1. busted   2. foreigner   3. *clumsy person*
LUNCH PAIL   1. bucket   2. *lunch box*   3. cafe
MOSEY   1. *to stroll*   2. to fall over   3. to sleep
NIGHT STICK   1. a beetle   2. whisky   3. *policeman's truncheon*
PAVEMENT   1. *the road*   2. the pavement   3. concrete
PESKY   1. furry   2. small   3. *troublesome*
PIZAZZ   1. nuts   2. *energy*   3. noisy

POOPED 1. cracked 2. lost 3. *tired*
PURSE 1. *handbag* 2. purse 3. plastic bag
SARSAPARILLA 1. a fruit 2. *a soft drink* 3. a town
SCHMUK 1. porridge 2. small dog 3. *nasty person*
SCUTTLEBUTT 1. *gossipy person* 2. run fast 3. a clown
SIDEWALK 1. helper 2. *pavement* 3. road crossing
SKILLET 1. *frying pan* 2. servant 3. a snake
SLAMMER 1. sail boat 2. shutter 3. *jail*
SMASHEROO 1. car crash 2. *big success* 3. drunk
TACKY 1. sticky 2. *shabby* 3. toffee
TRASH 1. cut up 2. *rubbish* 3. litter
TRUNK 1. railway 2. cardboard box 3. *car boot*
ZILCH 1. *nothing* 2. oil 3. grease

Check answers.

Further activities

1. Change the following to American English:

   My old car had run out of petrol, so I strolled along the pavement looking for a garage. A policeman eating a jam doughnut told me where to go. I was really tired by the time I got to a shabby petrol station. It was all rubbish and dustbins, and there's these two nasty blokes playing draughts in a backroom without curtains by a yellow coloured fridge. Beat it, they said, ain't got no petrol. Ain't got nothing.

   For a truly authentic flavour, use 'donut' and 'colored'. This may lead to comparisons of spelling systems.

2. Ask the children, when they watch American television programmes, to collect examples of American English.

4 Nice or Nasty?

Tell the children to think of someone very fat. What words could we use to describe that person instead of 'fat'? (Plump, stout, tubby, podgy, chubby, ample, dumpy.)

Think of words we can use to describe a thin person (lean, spare, skinny, slim, lanky, scraggy, willowy, slender).

Are any of these words nicer than others? If you were very thin would you prefer to be called slender or scraggy, slim or skinny?

If you wanted to be rude about someone you would use a nasty word; if you wanted to be friendly you would use a nice word, even though the two people were exactly the same size.

Get the children to sort the following into three big circles labelled **Nice, Nasty** and **Neutral** (explain 'neutral'). Work in groups or pairs.

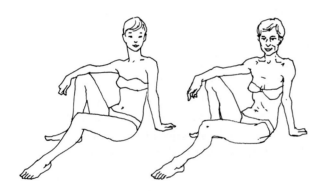

A. Words applied to people

timid, bashful, sheepish, nervous

cunning, shifty, clever, tricky, smart, wise, brainy

bouncy, jolly, pushy, good-humoured, free and easy

unhappy, gloomy, solemn, moody, grim, wet blanket, sad, depressed

ugly, plain, handsome, pretty, hideous, eyesore, stunning, beautiful, scruffy, dressed to kill, sight for sore eyes, face would stop a clock

Remind pupils that it is not whether *feeling* like this is nice or nasty, but whether it is something you can say about someone else.

B. Not applied to people

perfume, smell, fragrance, stink, pong

warm, sweltering, boiling, hot, scorching, scalding, baking

soft, mushy, squashy, doughy, spongy

sweet, syrupy, sickly, sugary, treacly

watch, gaze, stare, gape, peep, glance, goggle

glitter, dazzle, glare, glint, gleam, sparkle, twinkle, blaze

Compare sortings afterwards and discuss.

Note: the children will be visualizing the words in different contexts, and this will determine how they value the words. Explore this, and discuss the way that context determines meaning.

They may like the sound of a word irrespective of its meaning.

Further activities

1. Arrange these words in order of strength, hottest first:
   warm, sweltering, boiling, scalding, hot

   Arrange these words in order of the degree of praise when applied to someone else:
   brilliant, clever, brainy, bright, genius, smart

   Arrange these words in order of unpleasantness:
   chilly, freezing, bitter, cool, icy, cold, nippy

   Arrange these words in order of pleasantness:
   glow, shimmer, glare, dazzle, twinkle, sparkle.

2. Use a thesaurus (e.g. *The Oxford Children's Thesaurus*, Alan Spooner) to find nice/nasty versions for:
   cry (weep/blubber), ask (request/demand), drink (sip/ guzzle), question (interview/interrogate), eat (dine/guzzle), a crowd (gathering/mob).

3. You are writing a story. Write a description of a truly horrible character using as many unpleasant words as possible (refer to face, clothes, general appearance, voice and movements).

5 Puns

Give the children these newspaper headlines:

> Postman gets the sack
> Chip Shop owner battered in attack
> Cars stuck in jam

Explain that a pun is a word with two different meanings as it is used in any one sentence. Discuss the two meanings of 'sack', 'battered' and 'jam'.

Note: you can pun on sounds irrespective of spelling, e.g. cheap/cheep; bear/bare.

Now ask the children, working in pairs, to look at these headlines, identify the puns, and see if they can write down the **two** meanings of each.

1. Police hold man over fire
2. Fireman marries old flame
3. Wallpaper company takes a pasting
4. Train drivers' talks go off the rails
5. Shoe salesman gets the boot
6. Mothers who smoke have lighter children
7. Pub owner in bitter argument
8. Wages frozen for ice-cream salesmen
9. Plumber arrested with tap on shoulder
10. Gas information leaked
11. Bacon price sliced
12. Plans for new airliner get off the ground
13. Christmas snow on the cards
14. Cat owner's perfect holiday
15. General flies back to front
16. Belt up you drivers and stop complaining
17. Steak house waitress grilled by police
18. TVs weathermen left out in the cold
19. Two electricians charged
20. Prize budgies going cheap
21. Missing dog is spotted
22. Nurses upset by cuts
23. Top athletes lick Canada
24. Butter price war spreads

Further activities

1. Everybody brings a newspaper to school. Cut out suitable headlines and discuss any puns that you can find. You could start a class collection with a display. (This may provide an opportunity to discuss alliteration.)

2. Do any of these have double meanings? Say what the meanings are and make up newspaper headlines using some of them:

   framed, short pants, in the bag, get the hump, sees red, close shave, a screw loose, wrong end of the stick, panda crossing, loses case, lightning strike

6 Shopping

Remind children that many things you can buy in shops have the names of animals or birds: Penguin (biscuit), Lion (chocolate bar), Stork (margarine), Robin (starch), Woodpecker (cider).

Working in groups or pairs, ask the children to make a list of things you can find in a supermarket with names that have little or nothing to do with what the product is actually made of, e.g. names of animals, birds, flowers or emotions. Explain that these should be brand names not descriptions of the type of product.

Teacher can add to the list when pupils report back. Try to get the children thinking of the word name independently in its general use (this is not easy; advertisers have spent millions of pounds to prevent this happening). Using lower case initial letters for the names may underline this.

Teacher's list

ajax (cleaner)
breakaway (biscuit)
Biarritz (chocolate)
bounty (chocolate bar)
bounce (dog food, fabric
    conditioner)
buttons (chocolate)
black magic (chocolate)
balance (skimmed milk)
bold (detergent)
comfort (fabric conditioner)
crest (toothpaste)
choice (dog food, polish)
choosy (cat food)
Captain Morgan (rum)
camp (coffee)
chum (dog food)
club (biscuit)
carnation (milk)
cherry blossom (polish)
clover (margarine)
cheerios (cereal)
double decker (chocolate)
delight (angel) (dessert)
Earl Grey (tea)
echo (margarine)
fairy liquid (soap)
fern (tissues)
fiesta (tissues)

finish (washing powder)
flash (cleaner)
frolic (dog food)
Garibaldi (biscuit)
glade (air freshener)
galaxy (chocolate)
gourmet (cat food)
gumption (cleaner)
head and shoulders (shampoo)
haze (air freshener)
hit (biscuit)
haunted house (spaghetti)
harp (lager)
harvest crunch (cereal)
home pride (flour)
hula hoops (snack)
impact (cleaner)
invaders (spaghetti)
jump (cereal bars)
jackets (crisps)
kestrel (lager)
lifeguard (disinfectant)
lilt (drink)
Lincoln (biscuit)
marigold (rubber gloves)
minstrels (chocolate)
Milton (disinfectant)
marvel (skimmed milk)
Mars (chocolate)

marathon (chocolate)
milky way (chocolate)
monster (munch) (snack)
Nice (biscuit)
Norseman (lager)
orbit (chewing gum)
pal (dog food)
pampers (nappies)
panda (pops) (drink)
preludes (biscuits)
prime (dog food)
polo (mints)
pledge (polish)
quavers (snack)
right guard (deodorant)
red mountain (coffee)
roses (chocolates)
ritz (biscuits)
shapes (dog biscuits)
surf (detergent)
signal (toothpaste)
sure (deodorant)
seven seas (vitamins)
snowballs (mallows)
solar (cereal bars)
sparkle (polish)

skittles (sweets)
start (cereal)
space raiders (snack)
smash (instant potato)
sun (washing powder)
ski (yoghurt)
swan (matches)
(Mr) sheen (polish)
tunes (menthol sweets)
tracker (chocolate)
top deck (shandy)
topic (chocolate)
turtle (car wax)
team (cereal)
treasure island (spaghetti)
trill (budgie food)
tubes (snacks)
tip top (dessert topping)
united (biscuit)
vanish (stain remover)
velvet (tissues)
vortex (bleach)
waggon wheels (biscuits)
waistline (French dressing)
yeoman (instant potato)

After the first attempt to compile a list in the classroom, the children can be given a few days during which to look round the local supermarket.

Select some names which bear (a) a clear relation to the product (e.g. Trill, Pal) (b) absolutely no apparent relation at all (Echo, Hit). Discuss how certain of the names *might* be appropriate, encouraging the children to make connections.

Ask the children to think of good brand names for a selection of products, e.g. porridge, tea, glue, parrot food, a new squash, a new detergent.

Ask the children to suggest products that could have the following brand names:

Surrender
Force
Armadillos
Eagle
Doorknobs
Snooze
Hercules
Hint

Belch
Nightingale
Blunder
Wrinkles
Pirate
Megaphone
Goalkeepers
Attila

7 Days and Months

Ask the children where they have seen this sequence before:

> Sun Moon Tiu Woden Thor Freya Saturn

If they give up, give them this clue: put 'day' after each.

Tell the children the stories of these characters. (Sun and Moon explain themselves.)

Tiu (or Tyr)

The Norse god of war. Son of Odin, king of the Norse gods. Carried a huge sword. His great feat was to bind the wolf, Fenris. Odin brought a great wolf to Valhalla, the palace of the gods. But the wolf grew to a monstrous size until he was bigger than the biggest giant, and no one could control him. Tiu journeyed down into the caves under the earth and asked the dwarfs to make him an invisible and unbreakable chain with which he could bind Fenris. The chain was to be made of six things: the noise of a cat's footfall; the beards of women; the roots of stones; the breath of fishes; the spittle of birds; and the strength of bears. The dwarfs did as he asked, and with the chain he bound Fenris, though not before the wolf had bitten off his arm.

Woden (Odin)

King of the Norse gods, Odin presided over earth and heavens from his throne in Valhalla. Each day Odin grew older, but each night he grew young again. He would send his ravens to all corners of the earth each day to gather news. There is a bridge from his palace to earth, which we call the rainbow, and sometimes Odin would come to earth. He had one eye. When on earth, he would disguise himself so that no one would recognize him. His chief enemies were the giants. Once when he was on earth, Odin met a farmer who was distressed because a giant was coming to eat his son. Odin made the son the size of a pin, and hid him in one ear of corn in the middle of a huge cornfield. But the giant found him. Then Odin hid the son in a bird's feather in the middle of a huge forest. But the giant found him. Then Odin tricked the giant into chasing him, and led him across a great quicksand where the giant sank and was killed.

Thor

The Norse god of thunder, and another son of Odin. He carried a great hammer which caused instant death if he threw it at anyone. Thor was so huge that he was too heavy to use the rainbow bridge from the gods' palace to earth. Like Odin, he was much troubled by the giants. A giant challenged him to a contest. Thor had to drink the contents of a great drinking horn. He half emptied it, but could not finish.

Then he had to lift the giant's cat, but he was able to lift only one paw. Finally he had to wrestle with an old woman, but she defeated him. Then the giant told Thor that he had been tricked. The drinking horn contained all the waters in all the seas of the world; the cat was the great beast that circled the world with his tail; and the old woman was Old Age, whom no one can defeat.

Freya

She was Odin's wife, the golden-haired queen of the gods, and goddess of love and beauty. She owned the most wonderful gold necklace ever made, given her by the dwarfs. It was said that it was her tears, which, falling to earth, turned into gold. Her chariot was drawn by cats, and her special bird was the swallow.

Saturn

Unlike the others, Saturn is from Greek mythology. He was father of Zeus, chief of the gods, and one of the Titans who ruled before the gods became powerful on Mount Olympus. Saturn is sometimes called Chronos (Time). He destroyed all his children (like Time), except Zeus. Zeus' mother hid him, and gave Saturn a stone to eat instead.

These give us: The Sun's Day; the Moon's day; Tiu's day; Woden's day; Thor's day; Freya's day; and Saturn's day.

Tell the children to write down the twelve months of the year. Point out that the names of the months also have 'hidden' meanings, though we can't be sure about all of them.

Tell them this story, then give them the clues:

An eccentric millionaire once offered a prize of £50,000 to the person who could discover why the months of the year were called what they were. Many tried to find out, but failed. At last a professor discovered some carvings on a rock in a cave in the desert. The carvings were clues, and she was able to work out why the months have the names they have. Can you?

The children discuss in groups. Younger children may need help by being told that the first three letters of words are important.

Clues

1. The first Roman Emperor was Julius Caesar. Under him the Romans invaded Gaul. He was murdered by Brutus. (July)

2. Musicians form groups called septets. Find out how many that is and count to a month. (September)

3. The Greek goddess of love was Venus. She was in love with

the god of war, Mars. He was the son of Zeus. (March)

4. Find out what all these words have in common: decimetre, decade, decimal. Count, and you will find a month. (December)

5. In Greek myth the god Janus had two faces, one looking forward, one back. One of his duties was guarding the gate on Mount Olympus. (January)

6. The next emperor after Julius Caesar was Caesar Augustus. (August)

7. Find out what these words all have in common: octopus, octave, octagon. Count and you will find a month. (October)

8. Mercury, the messenger of the gods, was the son of Zeus and Maia. Maia was the daughter of Atlas, who holds up the world. (May)

Note: The origins of February, April and June are obscure and uncertain. November is simply the Latin 'novem', nine.

The children will probably be puzzled by the 7th, 8th and 10th months. How can they make December the 10th month and still have twelve in the year? The answer is to end the year in February as the Romans did. Discuss the advantages of having New Year's Day on 1st March.

Further activities

1. Write out a new calendar, giving days of the week in order (Sun, Moon, Tiu etc) then the months (Janus, February, Mars).

2. Find out on what day you were born. Are you Sun, Thor, Saturn? Read or listen to the stories again then write down all the characteristics of Thor people or Sun people (dangerous, big, great drinkers, handy with hammers; or bright, sunny, early-rising, never out at night). Make the list as long as possible. Will Suns get on with Wodens, or Thors with Freyas? Say why.

3. Make up a story to account for February, April or June. The story must sound very old.

4. The words below all come from the names of gods, goddesses or characters in myths. Can you (a) work out the name of the character; (b) find out what the word means. (Clue: the first two or three letters of the word are the most helpful.)

   For younger children, give the list of names as well, in a different order.

   martial (Mars, war); *cereal* (Ceres, corn); *jovial* (Jove, king of the gods); *titanic* (Titans, the giants of Greek myth); *tantalize* (Tantalus, tormented by being forced to stand in water up to the chin, but the water receded every time he bent to drink); *vulcanize* (Vulcan, the gods' armourer); *chronological* (Chronos or Time, father of the gods); *atlas* (Atlas, who held up the world); *erotic* (Eros, god of love); *morphine* (Morpheus, god of sleep).

8 Noises

Ask half the class to write down noises animals or birds make (e.g. purr, grunt, cluck), the other half to write down noises humans make (e.g. shout, groan). Allow 10 minutes.

Collect all the words on the board in two columns. Possible responses include:

Animals howl, yelp, hoot, scream, gobble, chirrup, grunt, honk, bleat, cackle, chatter, snort, bray, coo, squeak, quack, squawk, buzz, roar, cheep, whinny, hiss, mew, neigh, purr, bay, miaow, trill, snuffle, cluck, croak, moo, low, bark, caw, screech, yap, cuckoo, cock-a-doodle, trumpet, twitter, whine, squeal, cry, scream

Humans mutter, shout, yell, cry, groan, whisper, scream, cough, roar, sing, bellow, snore, laugh, giggle, wheeze, yodel, hum, shriek, bawl, screech, wail, whistle, croak, grunt, cackle, hiss, whine, squeal, squeak, hiccup, snort, wail

Now discuss which sounds can be made by both animals and humans.

Game   Animal, Vegetable and Mineral

Explain these categories as: creatures, things that grow, everything else.

The children write down the three headings, then think of all the things that could make the following sounds and put them under the appropriate headings (many will go in more than one place). Work in groups or pairs. At the end, discuss their ideas.

groan (humans, animals, wood)
rustle (leaves, fabric)
murmur (humans, water, wind)
click (metal, wood)
splash (water)
tap (wood, humans)
slam (wood, humans)
tinkle (water, metal)
chirp (bird)
ping (metal)
roar (humans, animals, wind, water)
snap (wood, bone, animals)
peal (metal)
babble (humans, water)
clunk (wood, metal)
patter (water, humans)

crash (metal, glass)
screech (humans, animals, metal)
jingle (metal)
thud (wood, metal)
crack (wood)
slosh (water)
hoot (bird, humans, machine)
ring (metal)
plop (water)
chuckle (human, water)
crackle (fire, wood)
clink (metal)
clatter (wood, metal)
creak (wood)
moan (humans, wind)
gurgle (humans, water)
rattle (metal, wood)
swish (water, fabric)

Further activities

1. The teacher assembles a collection of objects made of wood, metal, stone, paper and foil concealed in a box. These are tapped, knocked together, or made to sound in some way. The children close their eyes and have to guess what each substance is and supply a suitable sound word.

2. Write two descriptions of the seaside, the first on a still, hot summer's day; the second with a storm raging. Include as many sound words as possible.

3. Working in small groups with tape recorders (taking turns if necessary) the children record a sequence of sounds which tell a story: e.g. steps along a road; through a wood; into an empty house; up the stairs; . . . climax. Give time to assemble sound effects. Write about it afterwards if desired.

4. Onomatopoeia.
   Which sound words try to reproduce exactly the sound made? Make a list (click, plop, swish, boom, buzz, pop, miaow, woof, moo, atishoo, heehaw, hiss, quack, cuckoo, fizz, thud, pitter-patter).

9 Signs

Signs aim to produce a specific effect in the person communicated with, and show a particular intention in the communicator. As such they are a good example of how language in general works.

Ask the children to think of as many written signs as they can, seen in towns, along the road, in shops. Collect a few examples on the board.

Now explain this classification: Commands (Turn Left); Prohibitions (No Smoking); Warnings (Beware of the Dog); Labels (For Sale).

Give the children the list below. Discuss the contexts in which they appear. Then in groups or pairs the children classify them under the four headings. Alternatively, with older children, do not give the four headings but discuss context, tell them to group similar signs, and see if the classification emerges.

> No Smoking. Beware Of The Dog. For Sale. Turn Left. Take Your Litter Home. Give Way. Exit. To Cabins. Queue This Side. No Dogs. Post Office. You Break You Pay. No Parking. Pay Here. Garments Cannot Be Exchanged. Vacancies. Reduce Speed Now. Private. Do Not Touch Exhibits. All Dogs Must Be On A Lead. Parking. Trespassers Will Be Prosecuted. Keep Off The Grass. Have Correct Money Ready. Use Footbridge. Open. Smoking Damages Your Health. Ten Thousand Volts. Test Your Brakes. X-Ray Department. Toilet. Fasten Seat Belts. No Standing On Upper Deck. Danger Low Flying Aircraft. Private Keep Out. Road Works. Closed. Fishing Prohibited. This Car Is Fitted With An Alarm. No Entry. Trolley Park. Late Arrivals Not Admitted. Pet Foods. Gates Closed At Sunset. MOT While U Wait.

Teacher's notes

1. *Commands*: Turn Left, Test Your Brakes, Have Correct Money Ready, Reduce Speed Now, Give Way, Fasten Seat Belts, Queue This Side, Use Footbridge, All Dogs Must Be On A Lead, Pay Here*, Take Your Litter Home.

2. *Prohibitions*: No Smoking, Private Keep Out, Keep Off The Grass, No Dogs, Fishing Prohibited, No Parking, No Entry*, No Standing On Upper Deck, Do Not Touch Exhibits.

3. *Warnings*: Beware Of The Dog, Smoking Damages Your Health, Danger Low Flying Aircraft, Road Works*, Trespassers Will Be Prosecuted, Garments Cannot Be Exchanged*, This Car Is Fitted With An Alarm*, You Break You Pay, Ten Thousand Volts*, Gates Closed At Sunset*, Late Arrivals Not Admitted.

4. *Labels*: For Sale, No Entry*, Exit, Private, Post Office, Parking, Vacancies, Open, Pet Foods, To Cabins, Closed, Trolley Park, Toilet, X-Ray Department*, MOT While U Wait.

*Some signs can be in more than one category: are 'Pay Here' and 'No Entry' orders or just labels? 'Road Works', 'Garments Cannot Be Exchanged', 'This Car Is Fitted With An Alarm', 'Ten Thousand Volts', 'Gates Closed At Sunset', and 'X-Ray Department' could be read as labels or warnings depending on whether consequences are recognized.

Placing the signs in the 'right' category is not that important. What matters is the discussion of meaning with the children, or *intention* and likely *effect* of the message.

In what category would one put:

Longford Welcomes Careful Drivers
Have You Locked Your Car?

Further activities

1. Who can collect most signs in a week?
2. Some signs, including shop and trade names, use 'phonetic' spelling, for example:

KWIK SAVE, KLEENEZE, TOYS R US, SNIP N CURL, PICK N MIX, KWIK FIT, BEAMRITE AERIALS, RITE FIX, THE LITE BITE, FOTOKRAFT, TASTY SNAX.

Collect some from the neighbourhood. Make some up.

10 Latin and Greek

Give the children the following list:

anti (Greek) against
aqua (Latin) water
arch (Greek) chief
auto (Greek) self
bi (Latin) two
bios (Greek) life
centi (Latin) a hundred
chloros (Greek) green
geo (Greek) earth
graph (Greek) write
hudor/hydor (Greek) water
ignis (Latin) fire
im (Latin) not
logos/logy (Greek) study of
magnus (Latin) large
mal (Latin) bad

mega (Greek) big
metron/meter (Greek) measure
micro (Greek) little
mis (Latin) bad/ill
mono (Greek) single
multi (Latin) many
oculos (Latin) eye
pedes/podes (Greek) feet
phone (Greek) voice
phos (Greek) light
semi (Latin) half
sub (Latin) under
super (Latin) above, outstanding
tele (Greek) far
terra (Latin) earth
thermos (Greek) heat

Give the children the following words; tell them to look at the key (above) and write down the Greek or Latin word that matches most closely, e.g. microscope, *micro* (little). Think about the meaning in the key and see if it helps us understand the English word.

aquarium, thermostat, chlorine*, phosphorus, mediterranean, misbehave, supersonic, centigrade, hydrogen*, terrace, magnify, supermarket, multitude, bicycle, ignite*, hydraulic, telescope, microcomputer, submarine, archbishop, anti-freeze, semicircle, malice, antiseptic.

Each of the following words is made up of *two* words from the key joined together. Tell the children to find the two key words and then write down exactly what they stand for in the key, e.g. geology, geo-logy, earth-study. Note: the words may not be exactly the same in the key.

telephone (far voice)
centimetre (hundred measure)
photograph (light write)
megaphone (big voice)
autograph (self write)
monocle (one eye)
geography (earth write)
subterranean (under earth)

hydrometer* (water measure)
antipodes* (against feet)
centipede (hundred feet)
biography (life write)
microphone (little voice)
binoculars (two eyes)
biology (life study)
thermometer (heat measure)

Now discuss the present-day meanings alongside their literal meanings.

Warn the children that not every word in the dictionary that begins with these letter combinations follows these rules.

Teacher's notes

- Chlorine gas is green (the children might also know 'chlorophyll').
- Hydrogen is the water-producing gas.
- Ignite. Consider car ignition (firing) key.
- Hydrometer measures the density of liquids.
- Antipodes, literally 'against feet' because Australian feet point towards ours.

Further activities

Amaze your friends!

Ask someone from another class how many words of Latin they know. They will say none, or perhaps try one or two strange sounding words. Tell them they know *at least ten*. Then ask them to tell you whether they have heard of any of these:

circus, vacuum, tandem, Fido (dogs), Astra (cars), Fiat (cars), Lux (washing powder), Status Quo, Ave Maria, Ludo, ignoramus, omnibus, finis, ego, genius, vice versa, memento.

If they say yes, tell them these are all Latin words *in their original Latin form*.

Circus (a ring), vacuum (empty), tandem (at length), Fido (I am faithful), Astra (the stars), Fiat (let it be), Lux (light), Status Quo (the existing state of things, no change), Ave (Hail), Ludo (I play), ignoramus (we are ignorant), omnibus (for all), finis (finished), ego (I, me), genius (guiding spirit), vice versa (the other way round), memento (remember).

11 Buildings

Tell the children that the following words are all parts of types of buildings. Ask them to find out what the buildings are, write down their names, and then put the right words alongside each. Work in pairs. Use dictionaries if desired.

dressing room, turret, observation roof, lamp room, smokestack, platform, keep, spire, ward, moat, helicopter pad, dungeon, cooling tower, paint shop, apron, day room, footbridge, hangar, dispensary, stalls, courtyard, wings, generator, font, theatre, spiral stairs, departure gate, buffet, nave, circle, assembly line, ticket office, stage, clinic, crypt, waiting room, pulpit, portcullis, packing shed, turbine room, gallery, footlights, sanctuary, canteen, vestry

Compare results and allocate harder terms with discussion.

Teacher's notes

CHURCH   nave, spire, pulpit, font, crypt, vestry, sanctuary.

CASTLE   moat, portcullis, dungeon, turret, courtyard, keep.

THEATRE   stalls, circle, dressing room, stage, wings, footlights.

LIGHTHOUSE   lamp room, gallery, spiral stairs, helicopter pad.

HOSPITAL   ward, theatre, day room, clinic, dispensary.

FACTORY   assembly line, packing shed, paint shop, canteen.

POWER STATION   cooling tower, generator, smokestack, turbine room.

RAILWAY STATION   platform, buffet, waiting room, ticket office, footbridge.

AIRPORT   departure gate, apron, hangar, observation roof.

Now add one or two more appropriate words to each type of building.

Further activities

1. Make a list of as many words as you can find that mean *house* or *living place* for human beings or animals.

   House, hut, mansion, palace, flat, cottage, bungalow, chalet, manor, penthouse, vicarage, rectory, manse, villa, shed, shack, inn, castle, chateau, hotel, barracks, motel, igloo, wigwam, tent, nest, burrow, drey, run, set, henhouse, sty, dovecote, stable, barn, kennel, eyrie, den, lodge, byre, pen, warren, coop etc.)

2. Make up a similar exercise for JOBS (e.g. doctor, builder, chef, fire-fighter, garage fitter) listing tools or dress unique to each. Present these in a mixed-up list to be sorted, and the occupations discovered.

12 Newspapers

Ask the children for the names of any newspapers they know. Draw up a list from the class (they will come up with some of the nationals and perhaps the local paper).

Discuss with the class why a paper might be called:

1. *The Times* (signs of the times, modern times, times past and present, keeping up with the times)
2. The *Express* (fast, fast with the news, very fast delivery, papers once delivered by express train, pun on expressing views?)
3. The *Telegraph* (the 19th century morse code telegraph lines, later telephone lines, vital to quick news reporting)
4. The *Star*, the *Sun* (bright focal points of morning, day or evening, shed light, things to follow?)

The object of the discussion is for the children to think about the name, perhaps for the first time.

What about these?

5. The *Echo*, the *Mirror* (reflect the world around)
6. The *Argus* (the Greek mythological creature with a thousand eyes, missed nothing)
7. The *Beacon* (bright focal point, everybody sees it, warns of events, gives light in a dark world?)

Does anyone know why papers generally are called 'the press'? The first printing presses literally involved pressing the paper onto the squares of type with a lever.

Now give the class the following list of newspapers:

The *Aberdeen Evening Express*
The *Coventry Evening Telegraph*
The *Glasgow Herald*
The *Guardian*
The *Manchester Evening News*
The *Arran Banner*
The *Watford Observer*
The *Liverpool Daily Post*
The *Bournemouth Advertiser*
The *Monmouthshire Beacon*
The *Financial Times*
The *Oxford Mail*
The *Liverpool Echo*
The *South Wales Argus*
The *Richmond and Twickenham Informer*
The *Birmingham Post*
The *Bath and West Evening Chronicle*
The *Wigan Reporter*
The *Observer*
The *Leicester Mercury*
The *Islington Gazette*
The *Peterborough Standard*
The *Camberley Courier*
The *Morning Star*
The *Birmingham Despatch*
The *Correspondent*
The *Eastern Daily Press*
Today
The *Sun*
The *Annandale Herald and Record*

Now, attending to the last word in each title (The *Banner*, The *Echo* etc) the pupils work in pairs to group the titles under these headings (use dictionaries if desired):

1. Either *People* (herald*, courier*, Mercury*, informer, reporter, observer, guardian, correspondent)

   Or (harder) *People who carry messages* (herald, courier, Mercury, informer?)

2. *Things that stand out* (sun, star, beacon, banner, standard*)

3. *Writing or sending letters* (post, mail, correspondent, despatch)

   *herald – reads public notices or proclamations
   *courier – brings messages
   *Mercury – the messenger of the gods
   *standard – a flag

Which of these is the most interesting name for a paper? Give each a mark out of 10 for interest:

The *Daily Mail, Today*, The *Star*, The *Daily Express*, The *Independent*, The *Sun*, The *Guardian, The Times*, The *Correspondent*, The *Mirror*, The *Daily Telegraph*

These are the names of some newspapers from previous centuries. Give each a mark out of 10 for interesting name:

The *Globe*, The *Porcupine*, The *World*, The *Flying Post*, The *Merlin*, The *Oracle*, The *Black Dwarf*

Further activities

1. Make up some good names for newspapers.
2. Find out what these newspaper terms mean: masthead, by-line, headline, leader, the fudge, the gutter, the splash.
3. Find out the names of newspapers in other countries.

13 Languages

Give the children the attached samples of writing in different languages, and ask them if they can tell what each is. How do they know? Can they pronounce any of it? Allow 10 minutes in groups, then report back.

Key: A Arabic, B Welsh, C Chinese, D Dutch, E Hindi, F Polish, G Swedish, H Greek, I Portuguese, J Russian.

The children are now going to make up some words in a language of their own. Tell them to make up words for:

the, a, cat, sat, sits, dog, on, mat, table, lies, lay, ginger, black, and, jumps, jumped.

Using the words, make up these sentences:
(a) The cat sits on the table.
(b) The dog sits on the table.
(c) The black cats sat on the mat.
(d) The dogs sat on the ginger cat.
(e) A cat sat on a dog.
(f) A table lay on the mat.
(g) A ginger cat sat on a table, and a black dog lay on the mat.
(h) The cat jumps on the table.
(i) The black dog jumped on the mat.

Teacher's notes

Discuss these aspects with the children first:

1. *Forming plurals*. In English we mostly add 's'. Do the children want to add 's', use another letter, or indicate plurals in some other way? (Discuss what these might be.)

2. *Verb tenses*. Sits/sat, lay/lies, jumps/jumped. Strong verbs in English change their roots; weak verbs change only their endings. The children's past tenses should not be totally different words from the present forms, but the same word with a change to root or ending.

3. *Adjectives*. In English adjectives go before nouns. Some languages put adjectives after the noun. Perhaps the children would like to put 'black' or 'ginger' after 'cat' and 'dog'.

Second exercise

Now invent a *new alphabet* to go with the new language and re-write some of the above sentences using the new letters. Letters needed:

A, B, C, D, E, G, I, J, K, L, M, N, O, P, R, S, T, U, Y.

A

أَضْعَافًا وَكَانَ يُطَالِبُ وَزِيرَهُ بِتَوْجِيهِ ٱلْأَمْوَالِ لِذَلِكَ مَعَ قُصُورِ ٱلدَّخْلِ مِنَ ٱلْخَرْجِ ـ كَانَ يَعْمِدُ إِلَى مَنْ يَبِيعُ فِى ٱلْأَسْوَاقِ مِثْلَ قِدْرٍ وَقَمِيصٍ خَلَقٍ وَمَا يَغْلِبُ عَلَى ٱلظَّنِّ أَنَّ مِثْلَهُ لَا يُبَاعُ إِلَّا مِنْ ضَرٍّ شَدِيدٍ وَإِلَى ٱمْرَأَةٍ تَبِيعُ غَزْلَهَا عَجُوزٍ فَيُعْطِيهِمْ أَضْعَافَ ثَمَنِهِ وَيَدَعُهُ عَلَيْهِمْ.

B

Ond yr oedd wedi diflannu cyn iddi allu gorffen ei brawddeg. Teimlai Ann yn euog ei bod wedi'i dal yn y gegin ar ei phen ei hun fel hyn, ond nid oedd raid iddo yntau ddianc rhagddi chwaith fel pe na bai wedi gweld merch o'r blaen. Ceisiodd ail-greu darlun ohono yn ei meddwl. Yr argraff gyntaf a gafodd oedd ei fod yn anhygoel o ifanc — tua deunaw oed hwyrach. Gwisgai gap stabal a wnâi iddo edrych yn ddiniwed fel hogyn ysgol yn gwisgo dillad gweithiwr am y tro cyntaf. Yr oedd yn denau a gwanllyd yr olwg, a'i fochau fel llymru o welw. Ymddangosai'n lloiaidd wrth sefyll mor ansicr yn edrych arni efo'i geg ar agor, ond yr oedd ei lygaid yn pefrio'n dywyll fel muchudd, ac yn llawn o ddirgelwch, neu ddiniweidrwydd.

C

学院附设下列机构：外国语言文学研究所、苏联研究所、上海外语教育出版社、上海外语音象出版社、上海外语电化教育馆、上海外国语言教学资料中心等。这些机构在培养外语人才、提高教学和科研水平等方面起了很大的作用。

学院与国外有着广泛的联系，目前与日本、联邦德国、法国、美国、埃及、加拿大、意大利、比利时等国的二十余所高等院校有密切的合作交流关系。

D

Het is een vreemde samenloop van omstandigheden die het Engels - taal van een bezijden Europa gelegen eiland - tot de meest gangbare wereldtaal van het ogenblik gemaakt heeft. Voor zover onze huidige kennis van de geschiedenis reikt, waren de oudste bewoners van de Britse eilanden Kelten, en spraken zij een taal die verwant was aan het tegenwoordige.

E

हमारे अनुभव से कहीं अधिक, इस संसार में अविश्वास, अशान्ति और अव्यवस्था है । एक मे एक बढ़कर भयंकर अन्धविश्वास मनुष्यों की बुद्धि पर आधिपत्य जमाना चाहते हैं । फिर भी हमें अपने इस निश्चय पर अडिग रहना है कि संसार का समस्त मानव समाज— मुसलमान और ईसाई, बौद्ध और हिन्दू सभी एक निष्ठा से सम्बद्ध संगठित रूप में रहें । उनकी इस समान श्रद्धा का आधार अतीत में नहीं अपितु भविष्य में—प्राचीन जातीयता या एकदेशीयता में नहीं प्रत्युत विश्व-समाज के महान सार्वजनीन धर्म के आदर्श में होना चाहिये, जिसके अन्तगंत सभी प्रसिद्ध प्रचलित धर्म शाखा रूप से हैं ।

F

Jak się już rzekło, w przeciwieństwie do tamtej matki Luzynianów, pani Benigna nie miała w sobie nic z wróżki. Szeroka, silna, podobna była z dala nie do giętkiego węża, lecz do krzepkiego, sękatego pnia. Choć karły nie budowały na jej rozkaz cudownie rzeźbionych murów, czyniła ona także swoje czary, czary zabiegliwej, rządnej gospodyni. „Pańskie oko konia tuczy" — toteż żadna niepogoda nie byłaby jej wstrzymała od codziennego obchodu dziedzińca i zabudowań. Szczególnie wieczorem i w złą, jak ta, porę, gdy zziębnięci ludzie robią, aby zbyć. Któż lepiej niż ona sprawdzi, czy trzoda spędzona z lasu, czy żołędzie nazbierane, pójło przygotowane, czy niedbałe dziewki

G

Jag såg honom på gatan för en kvarts timme sedan. Det ar en kvart över tva nu. Kan jag fa en kopp kaffe till? Den man, som du menar, bor fem och tre kvarts kilometer från stan.

H

συνάγουσιν αὐτὰ καὶ εἰς τὸ πῦρ βάλλουσι, καὶ καίεται. ἐὰν μείνητε ἐν ἐμοί, καὶ τὰ ῥήματά μου ἐν ὑμῖν μείνῃ, ὃ ἐὰν θέλητε αἰτήσασθε, καὶ γενήσεται ὑμῖν. ἐν τούτῳ ἐδοξάσθη ὁ πατήρ μου, ἵνα καρπὸν πολὺν ᵖ φέρητε· καὶ γενήσεσθε ἐμοὶ μαθηταί. καθὼς ἠγάπησέ με ὁ πατήρ, κἀγὼ ἠγάπησα ὑμᾶς· μείνατε ἐν τῇ ἀγάπῃ τῇ ἐμῇ. ἐὰν τὰς ἐντολάς μου τηρήσητε, μενεῖτε ἐν τῇ ἀγάπῃ μου· καθὼς ἐγὼ τὰς ἐντολὰς τοῦ πατρός μου τετήρηκα, καὶ μένω αὐτοῦ ἐν τῇ ἀγάπῃ. ταῦτα λελάληκα ὑμῖν, ἵνα ἡ χαρὰ ἡ ἐμὴ ἐν ὑμῖν ᾖ, καὶ ἡ χαρὰ ὑμῶν πληρωθῇ. αὕτη ἐστὶν ἡ ἐντολὴ ἡ ἐμή, ἵνα ἀγαπᾶτε ἀλλήλους, καθὼς ἠγάπησα ὑμᾶς. μείζονα ταύτης ἀγάπην οὐδεὶς ἔχει, ἵνα τις τὴν ψυχὴν αὐτοῦ θῇ ὑπὲρ τῶν φίλων αὐτοῦ. ὑμεῖς φίλοι μου ἐστέ, ἐὰν ποιῆτε ἃ ἐγὼ ἐντέλλομαι ὑμῖν. οὐκέτι λέγω ὑμᾶς δούλους, ὅτι ὁ δοῦλος οὐκ

I

Do assombro que nas almas lusiadas, audazes, cubiçosas
e rudes, erguera aquele mundo embrionario, oue séculos
depois ainda espanta e amedronta, não ficara linka nas
cronicas. Mas soube-se, sim, que indo Guerra beirando
uma das margens do rio.

J

Архитектурным обликом Ленинград резко выделяется
среди других русских городов. Ему не свойственна затей-
ливая витиеватость Москвы, нет здесь и специфически русских древних белоснежных строений, которыми славятся
Суздаль и Ростов Великий. Ленинград подобен строгому
дорогому полотну, в которое вкраплены яркие узоры. Не-
ожиданно из серой громады улиц возникают необыкновен-
но красивые здания — Исаакиевский собор, Зимний дво-
рец, Русский музей, Адмиралтейство... Город был сплани-
рован и застроен замечательными архитекторами —
П. М. Еропкиным, В. В. Растрелли, Д. Кваренги, А. Д. За-
харовым, А. Н. Воронихиным, К. И. Росси, В. П. Стасовым.

Further activities

1. How many languages are there in the world? Find out as many
   as possible and make a list. It should include these:

   Chinese, English, Hindi, Arabic, Bengali, Russian, Portuguese,
   Japanese, German, French, Punjabi, Irish, Polish, Javanese,
   Italian, Korean, Tamil, Marathi, Vietnamese, Malay, Spanish,
   Turkish, Thai, Greek, Urdu, Norwegian, Swedish, Danish,
   Dutch, Afrikaans, Albanian, Armenian, Balinese, Burmese,
   Czech, Inuit, Finnish, Gaelic, Welsh, Hebrew, Gujarati, Hausa,
   Igbo, Italian, Kikuyu, Swahili, Luo, Maltese, Maori, Navaho,
   Ndebele, Santali, Sinhalese, Slovak, Xhosa, Yoruba

   For a full list of nearly one thousand languages with geo-
   graphical location and estimated number of speakers see David
   Crystal *The Cambridge Encyclopaedia of Language*, Appendix 3.

   Draw a world map and indicate with labels and arrows where
   the main languages are to be found.

2. Arrange these languages in order of the number of speakers:

Italian 60 million	Russian 150 million
Hindi 200 million	English 350 million
French 70 million	Japanese 120 million
Spanish 250 million	German 100 million
Chinese 1000 million	Punjabi 70 million

3. *Alphabets*. Introduce the class to the following letters and
   sound signs. Then tell them to try out the words given using
   the correct script.

GREEK (lower case)		RUSSIAN (capitals)		PUNJABI (the vowel sound is included in the consonant sign)
a	α	A	А	D ਡ
g	γ	B	Б	Go ਗ
d	δ	V	В	{ HE ਹ
e	ε	G	Г	{ HU
th	θ	D	Д	{ MA ਮ
i	ι	E	З	{ MU
k	κ	I	И	P ਪ
l	λ	K	К	R ਰ
m	μ	L	Л	Roo ਰੂ
n	ν	M	М	{ SI ਸ
short o	o	N	Н	{ SU
p	π	O	О	T ਟ
r	ρ	R	Р	
s	ς	S	С	
t	τ	oo	У	
u	υ	F	Ф	
ph	φ	sh	Ш	
ch	χ	u	Ю	
long o	ω			

letters are joined by a horizontal top line e.g: ਡੂ

WORDS

GREEK	RUSSIAN	PUNJABI
man	love	sir
thank	fish	sip
stun	room	her
mill	god	mud
rope	lake	map
dog	bad	mad
chorus	ill	sup
photo	cross	got
	dune	god
		hug
		root

Note: This is a game with scripts, and does not reflect the structure, vocabulary, pronunciation or word formation of the languages concerned.

14 Sounds Like . . .

Divide the class into teams of three or four children each. Explain what a homophone is, two words meaning two different things but sounding the same, e.g. maze/maize.

Teacher pronounces a word clearly and distinctly to the first team. The team has 20 seconds to write down two possible words. These must be spelt correctly to score. After 20 seconds the team gives its word(s). Score 1 for one word, 3 for two. Go on to next team.

Examples

meet/meat
father/farther
great/grate
peal/peel
place/plaice
flea/flee
cheap/cheep
tail/tale
steel/steal
male/mail
stair/stare
road/rode
pore/pour/poor
vale/veil
deer/dear
pale/pail
hay/hey
hair/hare
bare/bear
dew/due

weather/whether
rain/reign
peace/piece
foul/fowl
alter/altar
dough/doe
sell/cell
rough/ruff
bolder/boulder
sure/shore
board/bored
sail/sale
not/knot
mist/missed
shoot/chute
him/hymn
creak/creek
horse/hoarse
flower/flour
pair/pear

Further activities

(1) is easier than (2).

1. Find one word that sounds the same as the word given but means what is bracketed.

    (a) fare (place with swings and roundabouts)
    (b) fate (held outdoors in summer)
    (c) right (do this with a pen)
    (d) pain (piece of glass)
    (e) main (lions have them)
    (f) kernel (army officer)
    (g) signet (baby swan)
    (h) conquer (horse chestnut fruit)
    (i) peek (top of a mountain)
    (j) freeze (picture strip around the wall)

    Correct spellings please.

2. Find two words that sound the same and mean the following:

    (a) food/a place with swings and roundabouts
    (b) future destiny/held outdoors in summer
    (c) opposite of left/do this with a pen
    (d) anguish/piece of glass
    (e) water pipe/lions have them
    (f) centre of a nut/army officer
    (g) type of ring/baby swan
    (h) what King William I did/horse chestnut fruit
    (i) look quickly/top of a mountain
    (j) what water does to become ice/picture strip around the wall

15 Word Sets

We use words to organize the world. We classify the world by using classes and systems based on words, and the organization is 'vertical'.

The titles *The Times*, The *Daily Mirror*, *Stig of the Dump* and *Oliver Twist* fall into a two-part classification NEWSPAPERS and BOOKS. This in turn comes under the third, over all heading of PRINTED MATTER.

This can be set out in a tree diagram.

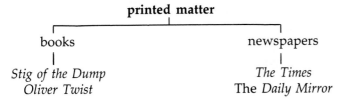

printed matter

books	newspapers
Stig of the Dump	*The Times*
Oliver Twist	The *Daily Mirror*

Talk this example through with the children, then ask them to draw similar trees on three levels for the following (work in pairs or groups):

1. ice cream, Christmas pud, lamb, tomatoes, pork, jelly, beef, carrots, cabbage, chicken, potatoes, chocolate biscuits.
This gives:

food

sweet	meat	vegetables
ice cream	lamb	tomatoes
Christmas pud	pork	carrots
jelly	beef	cabbage
biscuits	chicken	potatoes

2. violin, trumpet, harp, cymbal, cello, oboe, drum, flute, guitar, xylophone, triangle, trombone.
This gives:

instruments

stringed	percussion	wind
violin	cymbal	trumpet
harp	drum	oboe
cello	xylophone	flute
guitar	triangle	trombone

3. tennis, running, swimming, football, badminton, bowls, golf, javelin.

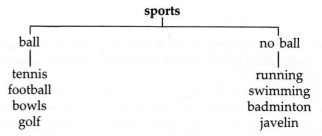

4. kennel, igloo, cottage, drey, teepee, set, warren, bungalow.

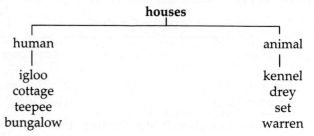

5. Mini, Concorde, liner, tanker, jumbo jet, Porsche, ferry, Ford Fiesta, helicopter.

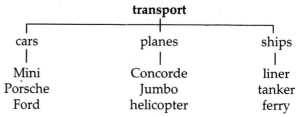

Once the game is understood the children might like to try more complicated ones, using more than three layers.

6. fir tree, mango, beetroot, banana, oak, cabbage, apple, yew tree, pear, potato, horse chestnut, spinach, plum, lettuce, carrot.

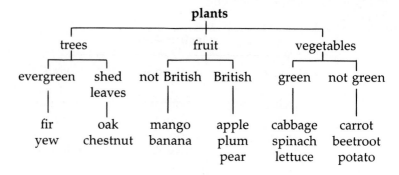

16 The French Connection*

When William conquered England in 1066 and made himself king, he brought the French language with him. For over 200 years French was the language spoken by the king, his barons and the powerful people in the kingdom. Because of this thousands of French words were added to the English language and we still use these words today.

Give the children this list of French words and tell them to write alongside each the English version we use. Work in pairs and *say* the French word; the sound is the best clue. Many of the words describe things to eat or drink, places or buildings.

French	English
pêche	(peach)
parc	(park)
cidre	(cider)
lac	(lake)
mouton	(mutton)
banque	(bank)
oignon	(onion)
crème	(cream)
aéroport	(airport)
concombre	(cucumber)
saucisse	(sausage)
moutarde	(mustard)
île	(isle)
oncle	(uncle)
parfum	(perfume)
sucre	(sugar)
porc	(pork)
hôpital	(hospital)
ballon	(balloon)
saumon	(salmon)
café	(cafe)
miroir	(mirror)
vinaigre	(vinegar)
boeuf	(beef)
forêt	(forest)
palais	(palace)
riz	(rice)
carotte	(carrot)
champagne	(champagne)
jus	(juice)
ferme	(farm)
restaurant	(restaurant)
omelette	(omelette)
hôtel	(hotel)

*Children learning French may find this too easy.

Now explain that in all cases the English word *is* the French word, derived directly. The pronunciation has changed, and some letters may have been moved around, but these are the same words. In some cases (e.g. omelette, cafe) nothing has been changed.

Further activities

1. Find a rule to identify French words. Sometimes it is easy to tell if a word was originally French because certain patterns of letters are repeated. Give the following list and ask the children to find *four rules* that will explain the shape and sounds of the words:

beret	reasonable
silhouette	buffet
amiable	possible
duvet	ricochet
brunette	terrible
horrible	etiquette
notable	parquet
serviette	pirouette
depot	ballet

Look up in a dictionary any words that are not understood. Give the clue to concentrate on endings, if necessary. The four rules are:

1. ends in ette
2. ends in *silent* t (not just t)
3. ends in able
4. ends in ible

Now apply these rules to find other French-originating words.

2. Find out if the following words are French in origin (use a good dictionary):

menu, chauffeur, blancmange, eclair, fete, chef, fiancee, suede, rouge, soup.

(All are French derived.)

17 Beasts

Give the children the following list of fabulous creatures' names:

The BONGALOO, the BOGUS BOO, the SNARK, the DOZE, the WENDIGO, the BANDERSNATCH, the WIGGLEWOGGLE, the MARROG, the GOFONGO, the HIPPORHINOSTRICOW, the QUANGLE WANGLE, the PUSHMEPULLYU, the UGSTABUGGLE, the NONNY, the JABBERWOCK, the SPANGLED PANDEMONIUM, the SNITTERJIPE, the HIPPOCRUMP, the TIGEROCEROS, the TRIANTIWONTIGONGOLOPE, the POBBLE, the YONGHY-BONGHY-BO, the JUMBLIES, the CATTIPOCE.

Say the names over slowly and carefully several times to get the flavour. Listen to the sounds. Does 'Snark' sound sneery and mean? Is 'Doze' slow, heavy and feeble? Sounds can tell you a lot about character. Does the animal sound nice or nasty? Large or small? Slow or fast? Fat or thin? Fierce or timid? Discuss some of the names in groups or pairs.

Choose three or four creatures and write down for each one words to describe (a) its size (b) its colour (c) any strange features (d) noises it makes (e) where it likes to live (f) peculiar habits (g) how fierce it is (h) behaviour when approached (i) its food (j) likes and dislikes (k) its hobbies.

Then get the children to invent a fabulous creature of their own. Give it a name, describe it, perhaps draw a picture.

Then read some of the poems which feature strange beasts. See *Prefabulous Animiles*, James Reeves (Heinemann); and *Amazing Monsters* ed Robert Fisher, (Faber).
(*Acknowledgements to Thomas Hood, Edward Lear, Lewis Carroll, Ogden Nash, James Reeves, Spike Milligan, Hugh Lofting, R C Scriven, C J Dennis, Palmer Brown, Peter Wesley-Smith.*)

18 Scrabble

Explain to the children how Scrabble is played. Individual letters are used to make a crossword pattern. The object is to use up your letters. You can make a word out of a word your opponent has already put down.

Tell the children they are in the final of the galactic Scrabble championship. If they can use up all their letters they will win.

A Two letters left. Get rid of one to draw, two to win.

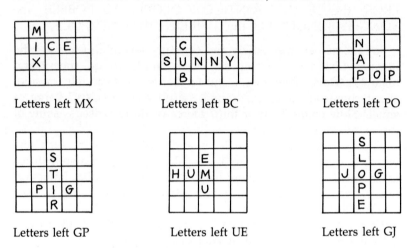

Letters left MX   Letters left BC   Letters left PO

Letters left GP   Letters left UE   Letters left GJ

B Three letters left. Get rid of one to lose, two to draw, three to win.

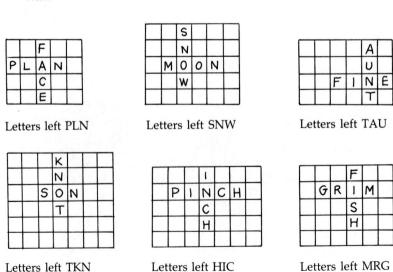

Letters left PLN   Letters left SNW   Letters left TAU

Letters left TKN   Letters left HIC   Letters left MRG

C Four letters left. Get rid of three to draw, four to win.

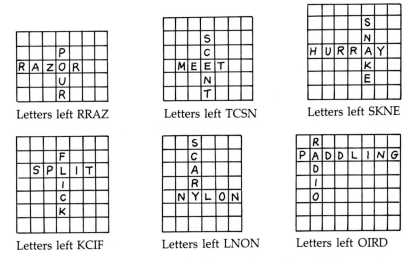

Letters left RRAZ Letters left TCSN Letters left SKNE

Letters left KCIF Letters left LNON Letters left OIRD

D Five letters left. Get rid of four to draw, five to win.

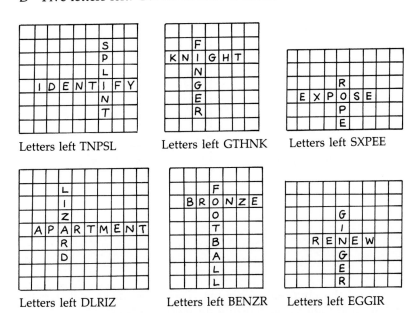

Letters left TNPSL Letters left GTHNK Letters left SXPEE

Letters left DLRIZ Letters left BENZR Letters left EGGIR

Further activities

The children may now be ready for the term 'anagram' if they have not encountered it before. An anagram is a word whose letters can be re-arranged to make another word. Give some examples and tell the class to make up some three-letter anagrams, then four-letter if they can manage it. Advanced classes might get as far as five.

3-letter: top (pot)   4-letter: mate (tame)   5-letter: cheap (peach)
       low (owl)   slid (lids)

19 Food

Quickly with the class list as many things as possible that we can eat and drink under the general headings fruit, vegetables, meat, desserts, confectionary, junk foods, snacks, biscuits, fish, soft drinks etc.

Now give the children this list of words which describes *taste* and *feel* of food and drink. Using the grid, the children work in pairs or groups to sort the words into categories.

delicious, yummy, sour, sweet, scrumptious, juicy, dry, soft, mushy, tart, gristly, pulpy, crisp, tender, raw, rare, burnt, lumpy, hot, cold, cool, runny, congealed, crunchy, oily, greasy, smooth, syrupy, crusty, stringy, squishy, salty, doughy, sugary, bony, gritty, bitter, chewy, tough, soggy, sharp, crumbly, rubbery, yucky, spicy, sickly, rich, fresh, stale, creamy, heavy, light, gluey, peppery, rotten, fizzy, velvety, frothy, curdled, mouldy, clotted, tangy, vinegary, luscious, succulent.

Nice taste	Nice feel
Nasty taste	Nasty feel

Discuss the children's opinions. Their placement will depend on the food they are visualizing for each adjective.

The children can then write a description of either the most disgusting and horrible or the most delicious meal they can imagine, using as many of the words as possible and using them to describe named foods and liquids.

Finally read the class the Centipede's song in Chapter 18 of Roald Dahl's *James and the Giant Peach*.

Further activities

1. (Easier) Many well-known expressions come from cooking or food, for example 'too many cooks spoil the broth' or 'your plan is half baked'. Can you find the meaning of some of these expressions?

> Leave them to stew in their own juice
> We'll have to cook up something
> I made a real hash of it
> You'll have to save your own bacon
> Spill the beans
> Know your onions
> It's a real dog's dinner
> That takes the biscuit
> My goose is cooked
> She's cheesed off
> Put it on the back burner
> Give them a good grilling.

2. (Harder) Can you think of any expressions which are applied to people taken from food and cooking and involving:

> stewing, hash, biscuits, geese, grilling, bacon, beans, onions

3. (Hardest) Can you think of any well-known expressions taken from food and cooking which can be applied to people?

20 'Old' English

The following extract is taken from an early best-seller, an account of a journey across Africa and India to China written by Sir John Mandeville in about 1350. In fact he stayed at home and made most of it up from the travellers' yarns that were then circulating.

Ask the children how they think 'old English' was written (with 'ye' and 'olde'?)

Give the children the passage and read it through with them. Can they read any of it aloud? Discuss what some of the words might mean. Emphasize that this English is 600 years old.

> Ethiope is in two princypall parties; and that is the *Este* partie and the Weste partie. And the folk of that *contree* ben black. There is a well that in the day is so cold that no man may drynke thereoffe, and in the *nyght* it is so *hoot* that no man may suffre hys *hond* therein. And the folke han but on foot. And thei gon so blyue that it is a mervaylle, and the foot is so large that it *schadeweth* all the body ayen the *sonne* whanne thei wole lye and reste.
>
> Fro Ethiope men gon into Ynde be manye dyverse contreyes. And upon tho *roches* of *cristall* growen gode *dyamandes*. And they ben so hard that no man may *pollysch* hem. And there growen many trees that beren *notemugs* and grete *notes*. And there ben vynes that beren grete *graps*. And after there is a lond all desert, where men may fynde no water for all *dyg-gynge*, so it is full of *dragounes*, of serpentes, and of other venymous bestes.
>
> Fro that lond gon men toward another lond, and there ben trees that beren *wolle* as thogh it were of scheep. In that contree ben many *ipotaynes* that dwellen som tyme in the water, and som tyme on the lond, and thei ben half man and half hors and thei eten men. And there ben many *griffounes* that han the body upward as an eagle and beneath as a *lyoun*. But on griffoun wil bere fleynge to his nest a gret *hors* or two oxen. For he hath *talouns* upon his feete.

Tell the children to write down the italicized words in the passage and put the modern spelling alongside.

Now write these words in 'old' English. Suggestions are in brackets.

fire (fyre), dog (dogge), fight (fyght), tiger (tyger/tygre), mud (mudd/mudde), house (hous), frog (frogge), iron (yron/yroun), fish (fissche/fisshe).

Rules: 'i' becomes 'y'; leave off final 'e'; 'o' becomes 'ou', double consonants.

Teacher's notes

Este (east))
Contree (country)
Nyght (night)
Hoot (hot)
Hond (hand)
Schadeweth (shadoweth)
Sonne (sun)
Roches (rocks)
Cristall (crystal)
Dyamandes (diamonds)
Pollysch (polish)

Notemugs (nutmegs)
Notes (nuts)
Graps (grapes)
Dyggynge (digging)
Dragounes (dragons)
Woll (wool)
Ipotaynes (hippopotamuses)
Griffounes (griffons)
Lyoun (lion)
Hors (horse)
Talouns (talons)

Further activities

1. Tell the class that spelling was not standardized until the 17th century and Shakespeare, for example, spelt his name in several different ways. This is their chance! They can write a *short* description of themselves using the most outrageous spelling they can devise. The only requirement is that the words must be recognizable.

2. On his journey Mandeville claimed he saw:

   giants with one eye, in their forehead
   men with horses' feet
   men and women who walk on their knees
   a great flowing river of stones, not water
   hens that are covered in wool
   houses made of gold
   trees that produce birds instead of fruit
   a lake no one can sail across
   lions with eagles' heads
   trees that grow out of the ground by day, but disappear
       back into the ground at night
   a valley full of devils
   goats all colours of the rainbow who keep changing colour
   mice as big as dogs

Using these and any other interesting ideas, write your own account of a visit to a magical island (use modern English).

21 Water

In groups the children make a list of all the things you can do with water. Allow 10 minutes. The groups report back. Discuss and add items.

> wash in it, bath, swim, drink, sail on, row on, steam on, heat houses, fill hot water bottles, cool engines, put out fires, grow plants, clean things, drive turbines, cook with, sleep on, baptise with, make steam for engines, soak tired feet in, use in water cannon, put flowers in, make ice cubes out of, surf on, ski on (wet or frozen), add to dehydrated food, make ponds or fountains with, drive mill wheels, water clocks, flush toilets, fill batteries with, paint with (water colour), float logs on, dilute things, find punctures, shrink things.

Now ask the children to think of the ways that water *moves* and of the *noises* it makes. Groups discuss and write down words under the headings:

Loud noises	Soft noises	Big movement	Small movement
splash	trickle	cascade	seep
gush	drip	spout	ooze
whoosh	plop	leap	trickle
slosh	patter	pour	dribble
roar	gurgle	swirl	drip
rumble	babble	roll	spurt
crash	murmur	race	lap
thunder	bubble	flood	creep
	chuckle	whirl	
		flow	
		tumble	

Compare lists. The children now write an unrhymed poem using this framework:

Without water we couldn't

2)
3 } List up to 12 uses, 2 or 3 per line.
4 }
5)

We'd miss its sounds, the way it

7)
8 } Give up to 12 sounds.
9 }
10)

We'd miss its movements, the way it

12)
13 }
14 } List up to 12 movements.
15 }
16)

Without water we couldn't

18 }
19 } List 2 or 3 more uses.

That's why it's so important.

The framework for the poem is only a starting point; children should begin to experiment with their own line order.

Further activities

Get the children to try out a similar exercise for *air* (uses, sounds made by the wind from breeze to hurricane) or *fire* (uses, sounds, colours, shapes, movements). Use a thesaurus as a source of useful words. Follow up with a free verse poem or short prose description.

22 Comparisons

Give the children all or some of the following list of similes:

1. His face was as white as paper.
2. The Queen frowned like a thunderstorm.
3. The Enormous Crocodile laughed so much his teeth rattled together like pennies in a moneybox.
4. And ice mast-high came floating by as green as emerald.
5. Mr Jeremy Fisher bounced up to the surface of the water like a cork.
6. The path twisted about like a corkscrew.
7. In the wood there were bats black as a top hat.
8. Bilbo was so hungry his stomach felt like an empty sack.
9. Stig's sneeze was like a cannon going off.
10. Frozen leaves underfoot crunched like cornflakes.
11. Their breath in the frosty air was like smoke.
12. We went to the seafront where we took a tram that shook like an iron jelly.
13. The baby held its arms and legs out like a starfish and snorted like a steam engine.
14. In the cold the birds were puffed up like woolly balls.
15. The goblin army advanced towards them like a tide.
16. The hurricane roared louder. The window shutters were bulging as if tired elephants were leaning against them.
17. Deep down in the ice were bubbles like cold green stars.
18. Catherine Wheels begin to flame like whirling marigolds.
19. The river ran through the valley like a silver snake.
20. The Wild Wood lay before him low and threatening like a black reef in some southern sea.

(Acknowledgements to Lewis Carroll, Roald Dahl, S T Coleridge, Beatrix Potter, J R Tolkien, Clive King, Dylan Thomas, Richard Hughes, Laurie Lee, James Reeves, C S Lewis, Kenneth Grahame.)

Explain example one. We wish to describe the *whiteness* of the frightened face. Paper is very white. So we use paper to give the idea of the whiteness.

The children should then go through the examples underlining the parts of the sentences which *compare*. Clues: they all come in the second parts of the sentences; they all start with *as, as if* or *like*. (Example 13 has two.) Check that this has been done.

Now discuss what some of the examples *mean*. How can a sneeze be like a cannon? How can a river be like a silver snake? What does the writer want to tell us by using these comparisons?

Tell the children that all comparisons involve two objects. The two objects are quite different but have *one or two things in common*. For example:

path
gravel or stone
on the ground
for walking on
can be straight
can twist and turn

corkscrew
made of metal
small
held in the hand
sharp point
its shaft twists and turns

sneeze
out of the nose
caused by dust
very loud noise

cannon
made of metal
uses gunpowder
very loud noise

Now draw squares for some of the other examples. List words that describe each object separately and see if it is possible to put down something that fits both. (Children work in pairs)

crocodile teeth
white
in mouth
pointed
rattle

pennies
metal
round
brown
rattle

tram
like a bus
on rails
seats
shakes

jelly
food
red or yellow
fruity
shakes

Now see if the children can think of some good comparisons *of more than two words*, the longer the better (work in pairs).

(a) The sea roared and crashed like . . .
(b) The wood was dark and gloomy as . . .
(c) Lightning zig-zagged down the dark sky like . . .
(d) Heavy snow covered everything like . . .
(e) My footsteps on the gravel sounded like . . .
(f) The witch gave a hideous laugh which sounded like . . .
(g) The monster's eyes gleamed from the back of the cave like . . .
(h) The rain on the roof sounded like . . .

There is nothing wrong with 'cool as a cucumber', 'hard as nails', 'deaf as a post' and all the other worn-out examples, but encourage the children to think of *long* comparisons, perhaps a line or more long. This will encourage more original thought.

Further activities

Read with the class some poems which have good metaphor and simile and discuss them. Good examples to start with are: 'The Flint' by Christina Rossetti, 'The Sea' and 'Fireworks' by James Reeves, and 'Cleaning' by Kit Wright.

Clive King's *Stig of the Dump* is not just a very good story, it also uses much non-literal language; flints poke out of the pit's chalk wall 'like bones', the birds are 'fluffed up like woolly balls', a fallen tree 'leaves an empty hole in the skyline', baby chicks are like 'yellow grains of sand running around' and a blackbird 'tries out his new spring voice'.

Tolkien's *The Hobbit* and C S Lewis's *The Lion, the Witch and the Wardrobe* also offer many good examples of non-literal language.

23 Machines

Tell the children that the following words are all parts of machines which you will find at home or which many people own. See if they can work out what the machines are (there are six).

Tell the children to write down the name of each machine and then put the right words alongside each. Work in pairs or groups. Use dictionaries if desired.

ribbon, chain, magnet, knob, handle, tank, keys, dial, fork, earpiece, element, speaker, case, battery, lead, frame, spout, platen, aerial, diaphragm, tube, wiper, spoke, radiator, lid, transistor, mouthpiece, space bar, clutch.

Teacher's notes

Radio   aerial, dial, knob, speaker, transistor (lead?)
Car   clutch, battery, wiper, radiator, tank, (aerial? keys?)
Typewriter   ribbon, keys, case, platen, space bar
Electric kettle   handle, spout, lid, element, lead
Bicycle   frame, chain, spoke, fork, tube
Telephone   earpiece, mouthpiece, diaphragm, magnet

Then write down some more appropriate words for some of the machines.

Explanation may have to be given for transistor (a tiny unit that strengthens electric current), platen (the roller taking the paper in the typewriter), diaphragm (the part that vibrates inside a telephone), magnet (which makes the diaphragm move), and element (the heating coil inside the kettle). If the children are familiar with computer keyboards they will know what a space bar is.

Further activities

Ask the children how many machines there are in their houses. Make a list.

> hoover, oven, electric drill, hair drier, record player, electric kettle, dishwasher, curlers, electric razor, paint stripper, phone, TV, radio, washing machine, fridge, lawn mower, coffee percolator, central heating pump, toaster, clock, sewing machine, typewriter, electric tin opener, car, motorcycle, cycle.

Then *either* (easier) sort the list into categories, e.g:

> Things that heat
> Things that cut
> Things that use water

Or (harder) Discuss whether these are machines:

> pliers, spanner, screwdriver, corkscrew, torch, water tap, door bell, iron, chip pan, sun glasses, biro, hammer, rake, spade.

Try to arrive at a definition of a *machine* and a *tool*. (A machine has many moving parts; get a machine going and it delivers the result by itself? What about manual typewriters?). Draw up a list of qualities which explain all the differences between the two (it isn't easy).

24 Clothes Stall

Tell the children they are going to collect things to sell on a stall. Not bottles, books or second-hand clothes but *words* for clothes. The idea is to collect as many words as possible and sell them for a pound each.

The words must be for things worn on the head, hands, body and feet, excluding jewellery, watches, glasses and hearing aids.

Divide the class into four groups. Two groups will try to write down as many words as possible for things relating to head, hands and feet. Two groups will find words for things worn on the body. Use reference books if desired. Allow 15 minutes. Then collect together each group's effort, and draw up a total list. This will indicate £x worth.

Then tell the children they have 3/4/7 days to reach a target of £50 or £100 or £150. They can use reference books, mail order catalogues, and ask around.

Display the final list.

Teacher's notes

Allow as many individual examples as possible, e.g. rubber gloves, leather gloves, woollen gloves. Clues can be given reminding children of jobs, sports, menswear, womenswear, armed forces' clothing.

The list may include:

anorak	boots	brogues
apron	– ankle	cap
balaclava	– army	– bathing
bathers	– climbing	– cricket
bearskin (busby)	– cricket	– flat
belt	– football	– jockey
beret,	– kinky	– night
bib	– moon	– peaked
bikini	– pixie	– school
biretta	– riding	– shower
blazer	– ski	– skull
blouse	– wellington	cape
blouson	bow	cagoule
boa	bow tie	camisole
boater	bra	cardigan
body warmer	braces	cassock
bonnet	briefs	cloak

clogs
coat
– fur
– great
– house
– lab
– over
– sheepskin
– tail
– trench
corset
cowl
cravat
culottes
cummerbund
daps
dhoti
dress
– cocktail
– evening
– maternity
– night
– pinafore
– sun
dufflecoat
dungarees
espadrilles
fez
flip-flops
flippers
galoshes
gauntlets
gloves
– boxing
– driving
– leather
– oven
– rubber
– wicket keeper's
– wool
gown
– academic
– ball
– dressing
– hospital
– night

guernsey
gym shoes
hat
– baseball
– bobble
– bowler
– chef's
– deerstalker
– fur
– panama
– picture
– pill box
– pork pie
– ten gallon
– top
– trilby
– woolly
helmet
– diver's
– fireman's
– miner's
– motorcyclist's
– pith
– policeman's
– soldier's
– space
hood
jacket
– bed
– dinner
– donkey
– flak
– Norfolk
– smoking
– sports
jeans
jersey
jodhpurs
jumper
kaftan
kilt
kimono
knickers
leg warmers
leggings
leotard

mac/macintosh
mitre
mittens
moccasins
mortar board
muffler
mules
neglige
nylons
oilskins
overalls
parka
petticoat
pinafore
plus fours
poncho
pullover
pyjamas
raglan
ribbons
riding habit
rollneck sweater
salopettes
sandals
sari
sarong
sash
scarf
shako
shawl
shirt
– sweat
– T
shirtwaister
shorts
skirt
slacks
slip
slippers
snood
socks
sombrero
souwester
stockings
suit
– G

- jogging
- jump
- lounge
- safari
- space
- track
- wet
surplice
swimsuit
shoes

- ballet
- casual
- high-heeled
- Oxford
tails
tie
tights
trousers
trunks
turban

tutu
underpants
veil
vest
waistcoat
wellies
wig
windcheater
wrap
yashmak
Y-fronts

Further activities

Play the identification game. Cut out a number of (clothed) figures
from colour magazines or mail order catalogues. Ask the class
how good they would be at helping the police identify someone.
Select a cut-out and walk around the class showing everybody the
figure close to but only for 10–15 seconds each. Then the children
have to give an accurate description referring in detail to the
model's clothes (oral or written). Be prepared for some odd results!

25 Cover it Up

Tell the children that people often try to make unpleasant things sound better by using understatement or 'nicer' terms (euphemism). They say 'passed on' instead of 'dead', or 'remove' instead of 'kill'. A lavatory (itself a euphemism) becomes 'the smallest room in the house'.

There are four topics which people are often unwilling to describe directly: being dead, misbehaving in a criminal way, behaving so strangely that they appear to be a bit mad, or drinking too much alcohol.

Give the class the following list:

Bats in the belfry	Well oiled
Turn up your toes	Fallen off the back of a lorry
A bit of a fruit cake	Bite the dust
Pie eyed	Lost his marbles
A guest of Her Majesty	Six feet under
A brick short of a load	Take an early bath
Round the bend	Lift the elbow
Drown your sorrows	A moonlight flit
The worse for wear	Three sandwiches short of
A knuckle sandwich	a picnic
Get a pine overcoat	Push up the daisies
A bit of a tea leaf	Curtains
Kicked the bucket	A screw loose

Working in groups sort these under four headings: *Death; Drunkenness; Crime and Imprisonment; Insanity*.

Further activities

Word maths.

Another way of avoiding saying something directly in English is to use the double negative.

Question: Is that true?
Answer: Well it's *not untrue*

This actually gives a slightly different meaning from the reply:

It's true.

The structure can be shown as:

Minus	*Minus*	*Plus*		*Plus*
Not	un	true	=	true

The class will by now be totally confused. See if they can put plus or minus over the appropriate sections of these sequences:

$+$	$-$ $+$	$-$ $-$ $+$
ripe	unripe	not unripe
$+$	$-$ $+$	$-$ $-$ $+$
stuck	unstuck	not unstuck
$+$	$-$ $+$	$-$ $-$ $+$
kind	unkind	not unkind

If they can, then they will be ready for the rule: TWO MINUSES MAKE A PLUS. So 'not unripe' means ripe, 'not unstuck' means stuck, 'not unkind' means kind.

Ask them to mark these descriptions with a tick for tidy; a cross for untidy:

tidy ✔
untidy ✗
not untidy ✔

Tick against which of these means 'well':

well ✔
unwell ✗
not unwell ✔

Now try and write down the three stages of *positive, negative* and *double negative* for:

plugged, raked, swept, made, popular

Finally discuss whether there is any difference in meaning between the positive and the double negative.

26 Animals

Remind the children that the names of animals and birds are very important in our language. Think of all the ways we use their names:

> It's raining *cats and dogs*
> A *zebra* crossing
> A clothes *horse*
> A *panda* car
> He's got eyes like a *hawk*
> He's bald as a *coot*

Give the children the following list and see if they can write down a saying, comparison or object using the animal or bird name. Rule out of order simple terms of abuse: e.g. 'rat', 'pig', 'louse', 'cow'.

bear (bear hug, bear with a sore head)
eagle (eagle-eyed, a golf score)
peacock (proud as a)
dog (dog house, dog's life, tail wag the)
horse (flog a dead horse, straight from the horse's mouth, don't look a gift horse in the mouth, put the cart before the horse)
rhino (skin as thick as a)
elephant (memory like a)
cat (cat's eyes, cat's whiskers, cat's pyjamas, forty lashes with the, no room to swing a, like a cat with the cream)
ostrich (stick one's head in the sand)
mole (inside the Secret Service)
parrot (sick as a, chatter like)
pig (greedy pig, male chauvinist pig, silk purse out of a sow's ear, pig in a poke)
sheep (the black sheep of the family, hung for a, lot of silly sheep)

sparrow (sparrow's kneecaps)
magpie (steal like a)
crab (walk sideways/crabwise)
turtle (turn turtle)
chicken (coward)
wolf (wolf whistle, wolf in sheep's clothing)
cuckoo (in the nest, daft)
beaver (to work hard)
bat (bats in the belfry)
hog (road hog)
leopard (can't change its spots)
rabbit (hopeless at a sport, to talk a lot)
crocodile (crocodile tears)
lion (proud as a, get the lion's share)
skunk (smell like a)
pelican (pelican crossing)

Further activities

As well as using animal names a great deal in our language we also give them some very strange names as pets.

Take cats and dogs as examples.

Either get the children to think of as many cat and dog names as they know and make a class list.

Or give the class this list of (real) names to sort into groups; (a) suitable for cats (b) suitable for dogs (c) suitable for both (discuss why afterwards).

Kitty, Fluff, Fido, Macavity, Tom, Ben, Pru, Tiddles, Orlando, Gus, Ponsonby, Prince, Daisy, Spot, Lulu, Harry, Coco, Tricky Woo, Lassie, Kipper, Smudge, Arthur, Fuzz, Blacky, Humphrey, Nipper, Crumble, Tosh, Buster, Vicky, William, Scamp, Yo Yo, Jackson, Kim, Patch, Sampson, Sadie, Tigger, Lucifer (pronounced 'Loose Fur'), Sheba, Mog, Growltiger, Sidney, Tabby, Sopwith, Queenie.

Then complete a class or year survey to establish the most popular/interesting names for family pets.

27 Compounds

The vocabulary of any language tends to increase all the time, although words are always being lost. This increase can be explained in several ways: 1.new words are being created 2.old words are being given further meanings, and 3.old words are being joined together to make new words.

Many English nouns are compounds: a combination of two words, e.g. penknife, teapot.

Give the class the following list in half-words, perhaps on cards, and all mixed up. With younger children indicate whether each half is the first or second part of a word. In pairs or groups, the children then see who can make most words within a given time. All the half-words should be written separately and without hyphens; there are no duplicate fronts or ends in the list.

arm'chair	tin'tack	goose'berry
rain'bow	air'port	birth'day
star'fish	pine'apple	moon'light
over'coat	wall'flower	sun'shine
green'house	post'card	scare'crow
bed'room	pan'cake	screw'driver
blue'bell	horse'shoe	foot'ball
dust'bin	news'paper	suit'case
house'wife	pig'sty	butter'fly
neck'lace	wind'mill	hair'pin
play'pen	life'boat	hand'bag
lamp'shade		

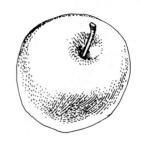

Further activities

1. Find some more compound words.
2. Giving the examples wellingtonboots, rabbithutch, tinopener, and treacletin get the children to bring in tomorrow's compounds *today* (why wait two centuries?).

28 Names

Give the children the following examples:

(a) Beatrice (happy) Barratt (cap maker) lives at Chiswick (cheese farm).

(b) Miranda (a wonder) Grant (tall) lives at Monmouth (by the mouth of the River Monnow).

(c) Philip (lover of horses) Higgins (son of Hig) lives at Swindon (on pig hill).

(d) Susan (a lily) Baxter (baker) lives at Oxford (at the river crossing for oxen).

(e) Iris (rainbow) Chandler (candle maker) lives at Chepstow (at the market place).

(f) Brian (powerful) Coleman (charcoal burner) lives at Bristol (at the place of the bridge).

Explain that all first names, surnames and place names *meant* something a long time ago, perhaps a thousand years ago. Some of the words were in Greek or Latin or French, or in Old English.

For example, 'Beatrice' is from the Latin *beata*: to make happy. Chepstow is old English for *ceap*: market, and *stow*: place. Swindon is old English for *swin*: pig, and *dun*: a hill.

The children may already know the meanings of their first names, and will certainly be interested to know them. The teacher should check the origins of these beforehand. These are some British examples (if children of ethnic minorities are in your class ask them if they know the meanings of their names or can find out at home).

> Alan – harmony; Andrew – manly; Alice – truthful; Dorothy – gift; Edward – rich; Jane – God's gift; Margaret – a pearl; Eric – kingly; Caroline – strong; Helen – bright; Peter – rock strong; Gerald – spear wielder; Vanessa – butterfly.

Most good dictionaries include a section on names; there are also specialist dictionaries of first names.

Some examples of British place names

Accrington – village where acorns grow
Beccles – pasture by the stream
Birkenhead – headland covered with birch trees
Bradford – broad river crossing
Cardiff – fort on the River Taff
Clifton – town on a hill
Crewe – stepping stones
Derby – village with deer
Durham – hill island

Ely – eel island
Essex – East Saxons
Finchley – finch glade
Hammersmith – at the hammering blacksmith
Henley – high wood
Milford – crossing by the mill
Norwich – north town
Penzance – holy point
Pontefract – broken bridge
Sandhurst – sandy hill
Sandwich – market on the sand
Staines – stones
Llanfairpwllgwyngyll-gogerychwyrndrobwll- llantisiliogogogoch –
St Mary's church by the white pool, hazel wood, whirlpool, and
the red cave of St Tysilio.

See *Concise Oxford Dictionary of English Place Names*, E Ekwall
(Oxford).

Some examples of surnames

Arkwright – maker of casks
Baker – a baker
Barnes – living in the barn
Capper – cap maker
Fleming – from Flanders
Green – living by the green
Grant – tall
Higgins – son of Hig
McIntosh – son of the chieftain
Saddler – saddle maker

See *A Dictionary of British Surnames*, P H Reaney (Routledge and
Kegan Paul).

Tell the children that most British surnames fall into three categories: 1.who you are son of (e.g. Anderson, son of Andrew. In Scotland this is Mac, in Ireland O'); 2.where you live (e.g. Green, lives by the village green); 3.your job (Baker, Saddler).

Give the children some or all of the following names and in pairs or groups tell them to sort the names under the three headings 1.Son of 2.Where you live 3.Job.

O'Connell	Glover	Brewer	Dixon
Potter	Churchill	Roper	Barber
Wheeler	Peterson	Lakeman	Fletcher
Ford	Fisher	Thompson	Brooks
Pond	Ashton	Thatcher	Pooley
Dawson	Cooper	McAlpine	Higginson
Leadbeater	Marsh	Caldwell	Woodhouse
Birch	Cheeseman	Firbank	
Lockyer	Ferguson	Macdonald	

Teacher's notes

1. *Son of* (-son, Mac - or O'-)

   O'Connell, Dawson, Peterson, Ferguson, Macdonald, Thompson, McAlpine, Dixon (Dick's son), Higginson.

2. *Where you live*

   Ford (by the ford); Pond (by the pond); Birch (by the birch trees); Churchill (on the church hill or by the church stile); Ashton (by the ash trees); Marsh (by the marsh); Lakeman (by the lake); Caldwell (by the cold well); Firbank (on the fir-covered slope); Brooks (by the brook); Pooley (by the pool); Woodhouse (in the house in the wood).

3. *Job* (all end in 'er' except Cheeseman)

   Potter, Wheeler (wheelwright), Leadbeater (metal worker), Lockyer (locksmith), Glover (glove maker), Fisher (fisherman), Cooper (barrel maker), Cheeseman (cheese maker), Brewer, Roper (rope maker), Thatcher, Barber, Fletcher (arrow maker, from French *fleche*: arrow).

Further work could be done on local place names. Many local historical societies have material on names. Local maps provide opportunities for place name study. Telephone directories are a source of local surname patterns. Check with the nearest reference library.

29 Horses

The names of racehorses are often evocative, imaginative or amusing. Give the children the following examples:

Lucky Charlie; Blue Spark; Silver Ocean; Island Pearl; Quick Mint; The Disaster; Golden Blaze.

Can we tell anything about the horses e.g. their colour or performance, from their names?

Give the children some or all of the following list. Working in pairs they must combine a word from the first column with a word from the second column to make up a good name for a racehorse. Any word can be combined with any other word in the other column, and perhaps some of the pairings could be left as they are.

Moon	Paint
Marsh	Glass
Blue	Sun
Razor	Wood
Little	Signal
Circus	Bear
Dragon's	Boot
Mister	Hymn
Crimson	Music
Sea	Kid
Royal	Cracker
Princess	Reef
Cool	Tailor
Harvest	Imp
Devil's	Mariner
Sand	Dawn
Snowball	Flame
Water	Bazaar
Super	Delight
Silver	Crash
Rippling	Visitor
Noble	Express
Gold	Bay
Orchid	Mittens
Star's	Warrior
Harbour	Strings
Bronze	Moon
Jolly	Arrow
The	Sharp
Night	Jim
Thunder	Flower
Indian	Isis
Crystal	Den

Cheeky	Rainbow
Mountain	Rupert
Tartan	Fruit
Prince	Castle
Abandon	King
Calypso	Hope

Teacher's notes

The originals are:

Abandon Hope	Moon Dawn
Blue Rainbow	Mountain Crash
Bronze Warrior	Night Visitor
Calypso Kid	Noble Music
Cheeky Rupert	Orchid Boy
Circus Bear	Prince Moon
Cool Sun	Princess Isis
Crimson Imp	Razor Sharp
Crystal Reef	Rippling Flame
Devil's Arrow	Royal Cracker
Dragon's Den	Sand Castle
The Fruit	Sea Flower
Gold Paint	Silver Strings
Harbour Bazaar	Snowball Jim
Harvest Hymn	Star's Delight
Indian Signal	Super Express
Jolly Mariner	Tartan Tailor
Little Mittens	Thunder Wood
Marsh King	Water Glass
Mister Boot	

There is no right or wrong about this. The idea is to get the children to experiment with interesting possibilities and perhaps stimulate imagination with evocative combinations.

Compare and discuss the combinations they produce (they will probably all be different).

Point out the alliteration in some of the names (Tartan Tailor, Silver Strings, Harvest Hymn, Calypso Kid, Dragon's Den). There are also linking sounds in some cases: Cr*i*mson *I*mp, H*a*rbour Baza*a*r).

Then ask the children to think of four or five new and original names for their own racehorses, remembering that these are racehorses and not pets.

Further activities

Word sounds. These are in order of difficulty.

1. *Alliteration*

   Get the children to write down a descriptive phrase with the same letter beginning each word e.g:

   > three thoughtful thrushes
   > a big black bag
   > glittering green glass
   > smooth salt sea

   Practise this for a while. Then tell them that it isn't the letter so much as the sound that matters, so 'Calypso Kid', or 'fine photo' will do as well.

2. *Assonance*

   Now write down two or three words that rhyme;

   > snail, trail
   > car, far, star
   > fish, wish
   > hiss, kiss, miss

   Then if possible (harder) write down two or three words that don't rhyme but have the same sound somewhere *inside* them;

   > c*ar*pet st*ar*
   > sh*i*ne gr*i*my
   > p*att*er sm*att*ering
   > gr*ee*n m*ee*ting

   Work in pairs; the first partner keeps saying the 'ar' or 'att' or 'ee' sound while the other partner tries out other words to make a match.

3. Finally, try to produce two or three lines of continuous description which make sense and in which (a) many of the words start with the same letter/sound; (b) some of the words placed next to each other *either* rhyme *or* have the same sounds inside them.

   Go back to the list of horses and find more sound links in the pairs.

30 Instructions

Show the children this drawing. Let individuals try in turn to describe the drawing so that someone who *can't see it* could draw it exactly from the verbal instructions.

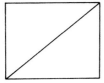

Now try this one:

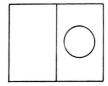

Check that the children understand these terms: left, right, square, triangle, rectangle, circle, horizontal, vertical, diagonal, base, half way.

Game

Divide the class into two teams. The teacher selects six 'instructors' in each team. The first instructor from Team One goes to the front of the class and is given a drawing by the teacher. The instructor, without showing the drawing to the rest of the class, must give clear instructions to his/her team so that they can reproduce the drawing *exactly* from the instructions given. The instructions must be verbal; no use of hands or other aids is allowed and there is only one attempt. The teacher then checks the drawings of the team and shows the original. For every perfect reproduction award two points; for something comparable, award one. An instructor from Team Two then repeats the process with another drawing for his/her team. The teacher keeps the score.

Examples of drawings (these can be modified to be more difficult or simpler as desired):

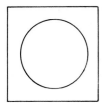 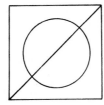 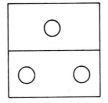

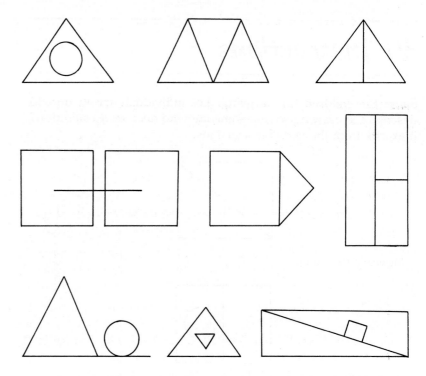

Instructions could be written or tape recorded. Give half the class one drawing, the other half another, then instructions on drawing are recorded. When complete, instructions are exchanged and attempts made to draw the other team's diagram.

Diagrams can be made quite complex if desired. Trial and error will show the point where the challenge is too great. Older children could try something like:

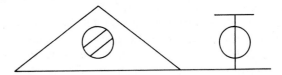

Further activities

1. Ask the children in turn to describe their houses (front view) so that the rest of the class can draw them accurately. Remind them this is a test of oral skills, not of drawing.

2. Using a book of world flags or heraldic shields, the children prepare explicit descriptions of individual flags or shields and read them onto tape. Encourage them to choose simple ones. The listeners then draw and colour the items. This can provide an opportunity to teach heraldic colours if desired; red: *gules*; blue: *azure*; green: *vert*; black: *sable*; gold: *or*; silver: *argent*.

3. This is harder. Describe a process or mechanism accurately using only words. For example, describe precisely a mouse trap, deck chair or canal lock including how it works.

31 True or False?

An interesting group of words in English derives from the names of people. Give the children these examples:

The sandwich: invented by the Earl of Sandwich in the 18th century, who was so fond of gambling he would not leave the card table and ordered his servants to bring him cold meat between slices of bread.

The wellington boot: originally long leather boots worn by the Duke of Wellington at Waterloo, later applied to rubber boots.

The children now play a guessing game in groups, considering the following statements and writing True or False after each (make it a team competition if desired).

1. The *biro* was invented by Laszlo Biro, a Hungarian inventor, in 1938.   (T)
2. The *saxophone* was invented by accident by a Belgian musical instrument maker Adolphe Saxe in 1840.   (T)
3. *Cocoa* was discovered by Charles Coca, a British explorer travelling in Mexico in 1720.   (F)
4. *Bloomers* got their name from Mrs Amelia Bloomer an American who first wore them to go to a dance.   (T)
5. *Cork* gets its name from Fritz Corkke, a German inventor, who made the first cork blocks in 1827.   (F)
6. The *leotard* is named after Jules Leotard who was a trapeze artist in a French circus.   (T)
7. The *diesel engine* was invented by Rudolph Diesel in Germany in 1892.   (T)
8. The *teddy bear* gets its name from Mr Edward Fawcett Bear, an American taxidermist, who made his first 'teddies' in 1901.   (F)
9. *Pants*, or trousers, were first invented by Eliza Pant, a Welsh missionary working in China in 1822.   (F)
10. The *hoover* was first made in the American factory of William Henry Hoover in 1908.   (T)
11. The *spanner* gets its name from Ramon Spannera, a Spanish car builder who made the first example out of a steel bar in 1863.   (F)
12. The *yale* lock was invented by Linus Yale an American locksmith. He got the idea from the revolver gun.   (T)
13. The *morse* code gets its name from an American painter Finley Breese Morse who invented it in 1854.   (T)
14. The *geiger* counter for measuring atomic radiation was named after a German Hans Geiger, a professor of physics.   (T)
15. *Toffee* was first made by Joshua Toff of Scarborough in 1798. The famous Toff's Shop can still be seen today.   (F)

16. The *umbrella* was named after Umberto Umbruella who first stretched canvas over a frame to keep the rain off in Venice in 1250.   (F)
17. Candido Jacuzzi built aeroplanes in America in the 1920s. When they all crashed he invented the *jacuzzi* instead.   (T)
18. The *tractor* was named after Peter Ilyich Trakkorski, a Russian engineer who built the first tractors in Siberia in 1917. At first they were known as 'trakkors'.   (F)
19. The *thermometer* was invented by Dietrich Therm, a Swiss scientist working in the 18th century. He got the idea from watching water boiling.   (F)
20. *Mackintoshes* or macs are named after a Scottish chemist, Charles Macintosh, who first made rubber coats in the 19th century.   (T)

See who got most right. Ascertain whether answers were based solely on guesswork, or whether some kind of logic was employed.

Do the children know any more words which are the names of people? What can they find out about the following words?

> belisha beacon (Leslie Hore-Belisha, former Minister of Transport)
> braille (Louis Braille, France 1809–52)
> cardigan (Earl of Cardigan 1797–1868)
> fahrenheit (Gabriel Fahrenheit, Germany 1686–1736)
> garibaldi (Giuseppe Garibaldi, Italy 1807–82)
> guillotine (Joseph Guillotine, France 1738–1814)
> pasteurize (Louis Pasteur, France 1822–95)
> shrapnel (Henry Shrapnel, England 1761–1842)
> stetson (John Stetson, America 1830–1906)
> volt (Alessandro Volta, Italy 1745–1827)
> watt (James Watt, Scotland 1736–1819)

Further activities

1. Think up some good stories which tell us about the (imaginary) people who invented the following objects which were named after them. Names, nationalities and details of discovery are needed.

> the jigsaw
> HP sauce
> spaghetti
> brillo pads
> bath buns

2. Does it sound better? Teacher or pupils make up *two* sets of 20
   cards.

	Set A	**Set B**
1.	The morse code was invented by	John Macintosh and should be called . . . (the Macintosh code)
2.	Bloomers were invented by	Lord Sandwich and should be called . . . (sandwiches)
3.	The hoover was invented by	Laszlo Biro and should be called . . . (the biro)
4.	The diesel engine was invented by	Jules Leotard and should be called . . . (the leotard engine)
	etc	etc

After the cards are prepared they are shuffled and drawn in turn
from two hats. The class must now note the new combinations and
use the new versions *for at least a week*; e.g. 'I'm just going to biro
the sitting room'; 'It's going to rain, where is my bloomer'. Queries
from puzzled outsiders should produce a detailed and articulate
explanation (oral skills!). The children will also remember the originals for a long time.

32 Endings

Give the children these two words and tell them to put as many different endings onto the words as they can to change the meaning:

walk   -s
-ed
-er
-ing

tall   -er
-est

Then give them this list of endings:

-or	-ing
-s	-ix
-int	-ly
-ed	-y
-er	-es
-am	urp
-est	

Which endings will work with the words in this list?

call, near, play, fish, pull, farm, sand, hard, poor, paint.

The class makes up as many variations as possible. Then ask:

(a) Which endings have been used most? (-er 9, -s 7, -ed 6, -ing 4, -ly 3, -est 2, -es 1)

(b) Which endings have not been used at all? Could any of these ever be added as endings to any English words?

(c) What happens to these words if you add -ing or -er to them?

taste, map, run, take, pop, jam, grin, dot, shape

Answer: the final consonant doubles and final 'e' disappears before -ing.

74

Teacher's notes

There is a rule for each if you think it comprehensible and worth passing on.

1. The last consonant doubles if the preceding vowel is *short* e.g. hop – hopping.

   The last consonant does not double if the preceding vowel is *long* e.g. hope – hoping.

2. If the word ends in 'e', it is dropped when 'ing' is added e.g. tape – taping. (There are some exceptions.)

Further activities

Long and short vowels. The children say these words aloud and mark whether they have long or short vowel sounds with a '+' for short and '–' for long.

−	+	−	+	+	−
grape	tap	rake	cap	rip	ripe

+	−	+	−	−	+
kit	kite	fit	pride	bone	tom

−	+	−	+	+	+
phone	hop	rude	mud	hut	spud

−
puce

What does addition of 'e' at the end do to the vowel sound in the middle of the word? Some children may tell you this is 'magic e' which they learned about at Infant School.

33 Cars

Give the class the following list of car names:

> Colt, Granada, Cherry, Sunny, Fiesta, Sonata, Bluebird, Pony, Accord, Mustang, Cortina, Prelude, Jaguar, Rover, Lancia, Dolomite, Spitfire, Cavalier, Victor, Royale, Viva, Prairie, Zephyr, Capri, Princess, Maestro, Polo, Scirocco, Golf, Sierra, Montego, Hunter, Silver Shadow, Corniche, Stellar, Panda, Sunbeam, Alpine, Horizon, Solara, Astra, Marina, Mini, Allegro, Maxi, Orion, Scorpio, Ami, Violet, Sceptre, Imp, Moskvitch, Scimitar, Micra, Rapier.

Tell the children that cars are named after exotic places or fast and lively things, or royalty, but can have all sorts of names. The idea is to make them seem powerful or neat or romantic so that people will want to buy them.

In groups the children see if they can put some of the names under headings. There is no right or wrong, and they will not understand all the names, but see what groupings they arrive at. Tell them it is the name that matters not the colour. An example to begin with is *Animals*.

Possible groupings might be:

Places
Cortina (Italian Alps ski resort)
Granada (Southern Spanish town)
Dolomite (the Alps)
Capri (Mediterranean island)
Sierra (high plains of South America)
Montego (Montego Bay, Jamaica)
Corniche (French Riviera coast road)
Alpine
Marina (Italian 'seaside')
Moskvitch (Moscow)

Animals
Colt, Pony, Mustang, Bluebird, Panda, Jaguar

Weapons/War/Danger
Scimitar, Rapier, Lancer, Spitfire, Hunter, Victor, Scorpio

Winds
Zephyr, Scirocco

Royalty/Power
Royale, Princess, Sceptre, Cavalier (?)

Games
Polo, Golf

Size and Shape
Imp, Mini, Maxi, Beetle, Micra

Happy/Lively/Celebration/Music

Fiesta, Accord, Viva ('long live!') Allegro ('lively, cheerful, gay' in music), Prelude (music), Sonata (music), Maestro (music), Ami ('friend' in French), Sunny, Sunbeam, Solara (*sole*: sunshine in Italian)

Colours

Silver Shadow, Cherry, Violet

Freedom/Distance/Wide open spaces

Horizon, Orion (stars), Astra (stars), Stellar, Prairie, Sierra.

Discuss groupings. Why should someone want a car called a 'Scorpio' or a 'Royale' or a 'Sonata'? Why are so many of the names foreign? What sort of car is suggested by these names:

Silver Shadow (silent, swift, glittering?)
Imp (small, quick, busy, friendly, good fun?)
Colt (young, fast, lively, lots of stamina?)
Capri (Mediterranean island, clear waters, sunshine)
Rapier (deadly, streamlined, shining?)

Further activities

1. Think of a good name for a new car which is (a) fast and sporty (b) a rich city limousine (c) a small town car for shopping.

2. Look at some advertisements for cars in colour magazines. What kinds of ideas do the makers want you to associate with their cars?

3. On a car journey make a list of car names, distinguishing between maker's name (Renault, Volvo, Peugeot etc) and the kinds of names discussed above.

34 *Technical*

Ask the children to listen carefully to the following words as you read them out, and to write down what they think you are talking about as soon as they know. Read the words slowly, with pauses between each.

> garbage, dump, boot, string
> traffic, bus, crash
> gate, address
> mouse, nibble, menu

If no light has dawned try again, then add, one by one:

> bug, floppy, chip, hack, program

(All are *computer* terms.)

Once the idea of computers has been established, ask the meanings of these in computer context:

> crash (computer fails)
> menu (list of possible activities at program
>   beginning)
> bug (fault in program)

Make the point that every branch of knowledge develops its own language and vocabulary. Computers are very recent, the microcomputer having been around less than twenty years, but they now feature strongly in business, science, mathematics, record keeping and police work. A new language of computers has come into existence in the last fifteen years. Like all new specialist languages the words are either brand-new terms or old words used in a new way.

Ask the children, working in pairs, to sort these computer terms into two groups labelled (1) Brand new words (2) Old words used in a new way:

> baud* dump modem* disc pixel* wand slave byte* fax* boot
> nest mainframe* flipflop kludge* degauss* bus wrap-around
> software* joystick back-up glitch* BASIC mouse

*new terms

Discuss findings.

Point out that some new computer words are obtained by putting the first letters of a group of words together to make a new word. Give these examples:

> BASIC   Beginners' all-purpose symbolic instruction code
> GIGO   Garbage in, garbage out (Feed incorrect figures into
>   a computer and you will get incorrect answers out.)
> LASER   Light amplification by stimulated emission of
>   radiation.

Further activities

1. Find some more acronyms (NATO, RAF, AIDS, BUPA, NALGO, SOWETO, FIFA, ASLEF, AMMA, ILEA, RADAR, BALPA, OPEC, UNESCO, UCCA).

   Or; give some of these and see if anyone can find out what they stand for. Make some up. (Think of animal societies, SPOT, Society for the protection of old terriers).

2. Look at ordinary words used in special ways by specific groups of people:

   > a soldier's *frog*
   > a glass blower's *glory hole*
   > a jockey's *irons*
   > a papermaker's *pot*
   > a lumberjack's *dog*
   > a pottery maker's *slip*
   > a golfer's *eagle*
   > a violinist's *bridge*
   > a steelmaker's *pigs*
   > a sailor's *housewife*
   > a gymnast's *horse*

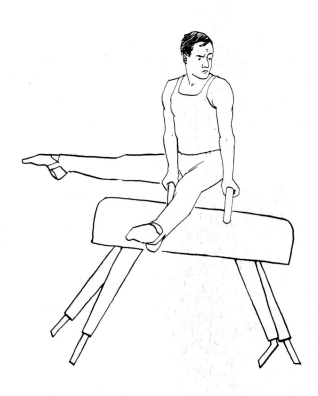

Teacher's glossary

address – a name or number locating something stored in the computer's memory.

backup – a second copy of a program made in case the original is destroyed.

baud – a measure of the number of signals the computer can deal with per second.

boot –to put a program into the computer's main memory and so commence operation.

bug – a mistake in a program.

bus – a link or circuit passing information from one machine to another.

byte – eight bits, the small unit of information storage.

crash – computer failure.

degauss – to unmagnetize a magnetized tape.

disc – on which programs are stored.

dump – to transfer information from disc to tape, or from computer to printer.

fax – facsimile; to send a picture or diagram along a telephone line to a fax machine.

flipflop – stores bits of information, changing positives to negatives if switched.

garbage –incorrect information fed in by the computer operator.

gate – a circuit that accepts electrical signals.

glitch – a small bug.

hack – to break illegally into someone else's computer system.

joystick – a small hand-held lever controlling some operations on the screen.

kludge – a computer made up of different bits of other computers.

mainframe – a big, institutional computer.

menu – the list of available alternatives displayed at the beginning of a program.

modem – allows computer signals to be passed along a telephone line.

mouse – a hand-held control box that moves the cursor or pointer on the screen.

nest – to insert new data into the middle of existing data in a program.

nibble – half a byte.

pixels – the numerous tiny 'boxes' or spaces on the screen that are 'filled' to make up a picture.

slave – a computer running under the control of another computer.

software – programs.

string – a set of letters or numbers typed into the computer as part of a program that is being written.

traffic – the messages being passed into and out of the computer.

wand – the 'pencil' used in shops to read bar codes.

wrap-around – feature which allows words too long to fit at the ends of lines when typing into the computer screen to be brought down to the start of the next line.